FROM BETTER...
to Worse!

A Memoir of Unconditional Love

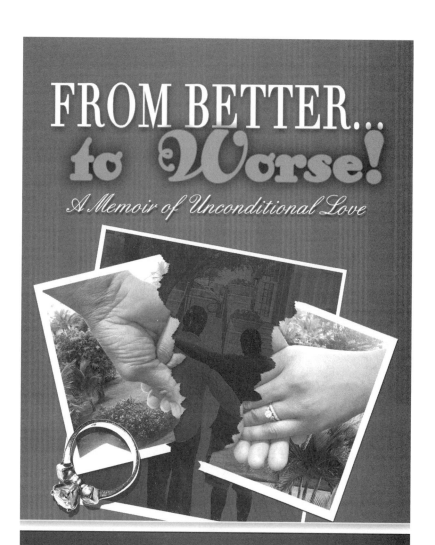

D. FELECIA WALKER

From Better to Worse:
A Memoir of Unconditional Love

By D. Felecia Walker

Foreword by Dr. Henry W. Foster, M.D.
Preface by Dr. Forrest E. Harris, Sr.

Dedication

This book is dedicated to all
persons in marriages and families
of individuals infected with AIDS/HIV.

Table of Contents

Foreword

Deborah Williams Walker presents a poignant and captivating account of a heart-wrenching life experience. She is to be applauded for so courageously exposing her most delicate inner feelings in telling this painful story. Indeed, this is, in actuality, two stories—one of tragedy and one of triumph. But beyond the gripping story itself, is the great utility this message holds for the hundreds and even the thousands of individuals that are or will find themselves in such trying circumstances that Deborah Walker has experienced. There are lessons to be learned from her story.

In addition to Deborah's strong spiritual faith and a solid sense of self-worth, the fact that she is well-educated was central to her surviving this ordeal. She chronicles well the sequence of her life events beginning with her courtship, wedding, and her marriage, before and after the birth of her son and daughter. At this point, life was beautiful for the Walker family. And then on February 14, 1988, this tranquility was shattered when tragedy struck with ferocity: Deborah's husband told her the painful news that he was bisexual. Although he had maintained an intimate marital relationship with Deborah, he in fact was what is now characterized as a "closet gay or bisexual" man. In the contemporary vernacular, this is characterized as men on the "Down Low" or "D.L." for short. These men have sex with other men while in sexual relationships with other women; thus the term "Down Low" equates to "in hiding." Following this gut-wrenching disclosure by him was a cascade of health challenges. He developed diabetes, then severe hypertension, and finally tested positive for HIV (human immunodeficiency virus). Subsequently, he developed full-blown AIDS (acquired immunodeficiency syndrome). This was a crossroads in Deborah's life. Guided by her Christian principles, the teachings of her mother and father, and the realization that her husband, despite his reckless lifestyle and its awful consequences, was the father of their two children, she formulated and implemented a strategy to support him in every possible way. This included interaction with his male sex partner, securing a safe domicile for him, providing transportation, and the provision of health insurance coverage through her job when he was no longer able to work. She was able to adopt and implement this course of action because of her humanity, intelligence, indomitable will, and the financial security that her excellent education afforded.

Though painful, Deborah did all that she could to make the remaining days of her husband's life as tolerable as possible. However, on August 11, 2005, her husband died. Although this brought an end to Deborah's physical challenges with this issue, her emotional challenges will remain with her always; however, she will have solace in knowing that she did all a human being could do under such exhausting circumstances. However, most fortunately, Deborah has remained free of HIV infection.

Although HIV/AIDS resulting from bisexuality is central to this story, it has, nonetheless, a powerful message for all families coping with the devastating effects of this horrific disease irrespective of its genesis. All who read this powerful story will be awed and grateful to Deborah Williams Walker for her strength, courage, and humanity. I thank her for sharing it.

Dr. Henry W. Foster, Jr., M.D.
Professor Emeritus, former Dean,
and Vice President for Health Affairs,
Meharry Medical, College and
Clinical Professor, Obstetrics, and Gynecology
Vanderbilt University Medical Center

Preface

When you read the life story of David and Deborah Walker, the reader can not escape asking the question, "What is the bottom line of life?" or "What is life all about?" Some thirty years ago at Harvard chapel I remember hearing the venerable sage of America's Protestant pulpit, Gardner Calvin Taylor, make a statement that comes close to providing a summarization of what our lives are ultimately all about. "Life is about success, failure, and God, there is nothing else; success that is sometimes failure and failure that is sometimes success and God." In later years, I found out this to be true. Success and failure are great impostors. What seems to be failure is often the pathway to success, and what appears to be success is sometimes a disguise for failure. To celebrate the life David and Deborah Walker knew together is to honor life's complexity in all its colorful mixture of success and failure but with God in the midst of them.

Life has a bottom line. It is a line vertical and horizontal. Drawn sometimes in complex angles, even in circles, no one's life is ever a straight line. As the pages of their story reveals, for the Walkers, life begins and ends with God. Without God, life is a tragic enterprise, an existential nightmare of broken promises, a sad symphony of rising and falling, a joy-stealing excursion providing at its end an isolated dwelling place of permanent aloneness. This is not the case for the Walkers and their lovely children, David Jon and Dannelle. God is at the center of the Walkers' story. Actually, this book is a strong statement of faith that says, "I lift up my eyes to the hills—where does my help come from? My help comes from the Lord; the maker of heaven and earth" (Psalm 124).

As the Walkers' pastor for nearly ten years, I have shared with them in intimate times of joy and pain. They lived in the blissful days of a happy and successful family, but they also endured the dark years of struggle against the HIV/AIDS disease that ultimately claimed David Walker's life. HIV/AIDS is a tough and merciless disease. The longevity of David's illness eventually wore thin the church's and community's compassion; but through it all, Deborah and the children stayed with David even when it was difficult to do so. You know when you have discovered what life is all about—it is when you can "love a person beyond their lovability." Without the help of God, this would have been impossible for the Walkers.

I believe this book will be a blessing for many families who need the company of a story like the Walkers's that can help them see God in the midst of life's failures and successes.

Dr. Forrest E. Harris, Sr.
President, American Baptist College
Director, Kelly Miller Smith Institute on the Black Studies
Vanderbilt University

Introduction

Commitment. One would ask, "What is it?" According to *Webster's Ninth New Collegiate Dictionary* it means 1a: an act of committing to a charge or trust; 2a: an agreement or pledge to do something in the future; an engagement to assume a financial obligation at a future date b: something pledged c: the state of being obligated emotionally.

Then another one would ask, "Trust. What is it?" According to *Webster's Ninth New Collegiate Dictionary* it means 1a: to place confidence: Depend in God to luck; 2a: to commit or place in one's care or keeping: entrust; b: to permit to stay or go to do something without fear or misgiving; 3a: to rely on the truthfulness or accuracy of: Believe; b: to place confidence in: rely on; c: to hope or expect confidently.

Someone else would ask, "Love. What is it?" According to *Webster's Ninth New Collegiate Dictionary* it means 1a(1): strong affection for another arising out of kinship or personal ties; (2): attraction based on sexual desire: affection and tenderness felt by lovers; (3): affection based on admiration, benevolence, or common interests; b: and assurance of love; 2: warm attachment, enthusiasm, or devotion; 3a: the object of attachment, devotion or admiration; b: a beloved person: Darling—often used as a term of endearment; 4a: unselfish, loyal, and benevolent concern for the good of another.

Commitment, Trust and Love: the combined definitions give us a sense of a sure thing. If we place all of these words and their meanings inside of a relationship we are bound to have a sure thing—no flaws allowed.

The problem about a definition is that it is only a definition to help us to understand how words are defined. Once one knows the meaning of these definitions, it is up to the individual to exercise the definition. We have a situation of which we know the meaning, but our humanness gets in the way and does not allow us to live out the true meaning inside of our real-life experience. This causes our sure thing to completely resemble something else that is all together different.

As we travel the road of life looking for some real meaning, we find varied ones. Experiences along the way cause us to look inside our relationships and the challenge of commitment, trust, and love. Can one hold onto all three when two of them have completely crumbled and the third is questionable?

In this real-life story I want only to give you the facts, the ups, the downs, the long suffering, the pain, the tears, the hurt, deep heartache, loneliness, and the grief. I pray that as you read the pages of this book you will not judge, try to figure it out, or question. Try to reconcile that God uses each and every one of us to spread our experience to others to allow them to understand and see His sovereign power through and within the human experience. I also pray that you see how He has a wealth of power and strength He provides when we only seek it diligently and are serious about just what we are experiencing. I hope you find strength, courage, awe, and the power to keep on keeping on no matter what the challenge or struggle is. As African Americans, our being alone is a struggle. We must and we will overcome some day but we must teach, work, be healthy, and hold on. We must hold on until our change comes no matter what.

The Courtship and the Wedding

When I graduated from high school, the church gave me a Living Bible. College days, college days: what fun and adventure! I entered the University of Arkansas at Pine Bluff the fall of 1974. I was so excited about being away from home (just five blocks away) and meeting new people. I didn't know what was ahead for me, but I was ready. I began my major in Institutional Dietetics after much encouragement. You see, when I graduated high school I told my parents, "No college for me. I'm going to the Air Force." Little did I know that my parents knew or went to college with all the administrators and professors at UAPB. They worked all summer, and when fall came I registered for classes. I told them that if I went there I must live on the campus, and they agreed. I knew if I lived at home I would never grow up because my dad monitored all guests (which I've found to be a good thing later in life). He should have, because he had truly been in my shoes in his young days.

The campus life was so full. I joined the Vesper Choir under the direction of Mr. Shelby McPhee, who was a church member and was glad to have me in his choir. When I went to the first choir rehearsal it was so much fun and the music we sang was literature of immense variety. Mr. McPhee always wanted quality sound, and he got it. We met daily, and this choir became a second family. We rehearsed most days from 6:00 to 8:00 P.M. There were occasions when we remained late because there was a large group of Memphis students who always cut up and clowned in rehearsals so we would have to sit quietly for ten to fifteen minutes past rehearsal time. I would be boiling mad because I had homework to do and I was ready to leave when rehearsal ended.

One Friday after rehearsal it was announced that there would be a party at Big D's house, and I thought, "Who?" My girlfriend April said, "We've got to go and check it out." I was so naive and she was also, but I knew she was from Chicago so I figured I could learn from her, only to find out she was as sheltered as I was. We still became best of choir friends and roommates later—for a short time due to the fact she could be real strange at times. She was constantly snoring, brushing her teeth all times of the night, eating and talking loudly. We went to the party and stayed only for a short period. I couldn't get over the fact that I was at a party with the students who made us get out of rehearsal late from time to time. The more I thought, I told April I was ready to go, and she never learned why we left so early because she had no hang-ups.

I was doing well in school and had no boyfriend and no one in sight. My home boy Joe Savage, who was in the choir with me, always looked out for me, especially since I had played ball and raced with him up and down my neighborhood street growing up. I felt like a little sister to him because he was always nice to me. Joe began pledging Alpha Phi Alpha in October 1974. On a Friday after choir rehearsal he asked me to round up as many girls as I could from the dorm and tell them to come to the fraternity house for a party. He said, "If we don't have that house packed out with girls, the Big Brothers will just punish us in an awful way." I went back to the dorm and rounded up all that I could. My friend, Carrie, from Gary, Indiana, was in the hallway and she was always boasting about her big hips being twenty-two on one side and twenty-two on the other side. She would always say, "And if you can't add, that equals forty-four." She was well-endowed in the hip area. I told her about the party and she said, "Okay." April came along too with other people I told passing in the dorm. We talked about how we would dress so we wouldn't look too much like fresh-man or "fresh meat," which is what all the boys thought about freshman girls on campus. Carrie was a loud talker so all you had to do was just be with her and nobody even noticed you.

The three of us headed out for the party. As we walked to the fraternity house we could see others walking and some arriving in cars. We all started laughing because we said that if our Baptist mothers knew we were going to a frat party they would kill us. As we approached the wood-framed black and gold building, the music was thumping so much that the window panes were moving. People were already on the inside dancing and rocking the house. We entered trying not to look so fresh. Immediately Joe came over and said, "I am glad to see you, and I can tell you spread the word." He asked me to dance with him, and I agreed. Carrie and April began to dance also. After Joe and I danced he began to talk to Carrie, and April was dancing with everyone. As I sat watching and listening to the music, one of the Memphis students came up to me to dance. It was "Big D," the young man whose party we went to the week before. I said to myself that one dance—just being nice—was all I would do. I was only talking to myself because he danced with me the whole night long. We said very little because I didn't like the Memphis students because they always caused us to leave choir late. I looked around and saw that Joe and Carrie were coupling but April had not made a connection. Dancing to a Marvin Gaye tune, bodies close, Big D began to whisper in my ear that I was a cute little thing and where had I been and he remembered me a little from choir. I was too afraid to tell him I knew exactly who he was and that he was a part of the group that made me sick. We danced all night and into the morning. He was a good dancer and knew all the new moves.

He got tired finally and we sat down and he began to tell me that he was from Memphis and that he thought it was fun being at UAPB. He said he wondered about the city at first because when they drove in it smelled so bad. I told him he had been introduced to the good old Pine Bluff Arsenal paper mill and, depending on which way the wind would blow, you could smell it anywhere. We laughed. I asked him how he liked pledging Alpha Phi Alpha, and he said they were very hard on all of them but he was going to try to make it. I told him I was thinking about pledging Alpha Kappa Alpha in the fall and that

I was really looking forward to it. We just sat and watched the others dancing, and he began to tell me about his health. He told me that he had a stomach ulcer and high blood pressure. At that moment I felt so bad for not liking him simply because of the Memphis students. I began to see him as an individual with individual needs. He told me he had been ill since age fifteen, and I had never met anyone with such problems so early. It was then that I feel I began to have some feeling for him even though I was still unsure.

Joe and Carrie came over after that thought and Joe said, "Let's take these girls home." As we got into the car to go back to the dorm Carrie sat next to Joe and I sat next to Big D. When we arrived at the dorm we got out of the car. I asked Joe if he would wait for me while I picked up a few things to take home for the weekend. When I returned we all sat in the front seat, and I was in the middle. Big D told me he was going home for a week to get some medical tests run and have high blood pressure checks. When we got to my house he asked for my phone number and said he would call me over the weekend or one day next week. I turned to Joe and told him I had had a good time helping him out and asked him if he wanted to race. He laughed and said, "Girl, get out of this car before your daddy comes out here." On that note I told them both, "See you next week!"

Big D called on Sunday just as he'd said. He just talked mostly about his family and getting ready to go to the doctor. We soon hung up. He didn't call again from Memphis. When he returned to Pine Bluff, I only saw him on the pledge line. The big day came for pledging to end, and they had the traditional Greek step show, showing off all the sororities' and fraternities' new pledges. The crowd was big, and the new pledges spread a lot of excitement throughout the crowd. People were everywhere just trying to see. When the Alpha Phi Alpha pledges came out, I had a front-row view. They were all so handsome and stepped lively. It was a special natural high. After the step show the Alphas had a big party at the fraternity house. Carrie,

April, and I went. We didn't wait to go and get anyone else; we just knew we were ready to go. As we arrived the house was full and already rocking with loud music and a big crowd. Joe came and danced with me first, and I congratulated him, and on the second dance Big D seemed to find me to dance with again. We danced the whole night once again. I congratulated him; he was truly proud, and you could see it all over his face. After a long night he walked me back to the dorm. I didn't talk to him much after that.

I remember one time when Joe and I were racing in the street, a bicycle hit me in the knee and Joe picked me up and carried me all the way home. I did think he was a little special then, but it wasn't a real feeling. Much to my surprise, I found out that Joe liked me. Later, I heard Joe had gone to Big D's house and told him I was his girlfriend and they had words (from what others told me). Joe never approached me romantically, and plus he was always my neighborhood and childhood running competition.

In November and after the pledging and partying died down, it was back to choir as usual. This time choir seemed different because Joe would walk Carrie to the dorm and Big D would walk me to the dorm. I wasn't really sure if I liked him, but he was slowly moving in on me. He would call me at the dorm and I would wave to him if I saw him going across campus or in the student union building. All in all it was just beginning. As I talked to different ones who knew him, they told me he had a girlfriend back home that he was engaged to and they were very close. After hearing about her I asked him about the girl he was engaged to. He told me her name was Bernice and that he was going to take his engagement ring back from her because he heard she was cheating on him. She was a student at Lincoln University in Jefferson City, Missouri. I told him I was sorry that happened. He just looked a little sad.

My classes were going great and we had several rehearsals getting ready for the Handel's *Messiah* with the Arkansas

Symphony. I always wanted to sing the alto solos, and when we had to try out individually I really sang to the best of my ability. Gloria Wright and Renee Brown were superb altos and upperclassmen so I knew it just wasn't my time yet.

Finals were upon us and everybody was studying and getting ready to go home for Christmas. Big D and I didn't exchange gifts, just cards for Christmas. He had bought so much for the previous girlfriend who betrayed him that I guess he was not going to invest a penny in me until he found out more about my character. He did call me once or twice over the Christmas break and explained to me that it was over between him and Bernice and that he had taken his engagement ring back.

It was the spring of 1975. Christmas break ended, and I was back to college life again. As soon as we had settled back in, Carrie said, "Girl, we need to pledge Alpha Angel since we are friends of Alphas and plus they are making a new line this spring." After Carrie convinced me we headed to April's room, and she didn't even think about it. She said, "Let's do it!" and we did.

Once we decided to pledge we told Big D and Joe, and it seemed they were all the more determined to be our boyfriends once they found out we were pledging. Carrie and I talked about them often, and we never really saw them—especially when pledging began.

During pledging we stayed together most of the time outside of class and choir. We ran errands and did chores for the Big Sisters. Big Sisters had so much power because you had to do what they asked you to do. Big Sister Davis came in my room and said to me, "Ah-hah! A television! I want it at my house because I don't have one." I almost died because my ninety-year-old grandmother had given me that TV. And it was the one she spent her whole life watching "Days of Our Lives" and "Another World" before her daughter replaced it with a new color TV. She gladly gave it to me because I was her youngest granddaughter and had spent a lot of quality time with her. I loved Grandma Cassie with her snuff-dipping self. We could talk about everything.

Back to the real moment: Big Sister Davis said, "I want the TV for the weekend." Everyone looked at me and how I was hesitating, but we all took the TV to her house and returned to campus. I didn't have a good feeling about this at all. As the weekend passed and Sunday came I asked Big Sister Davis for my TV. I couldn't be too aggressive for fear that they would not let me continue on the pledge line. She told me my TV was gone forever. Someone had stolen it. I was so sick inside, and I felt I had lost a big part of me, part of history, and certainly memories of hours in front of that TV. (I'm tearing up now just writing about it.) When she left the room the other pledges cried with me and wondered how I would tell my parents what had happened to the TV. After all, I would be moving home from the dorm for the summer. After that all the other pledges went and hid all their belongings that they thought a Big Sister would want to take.

The weeks of pledging flew by, and we selected our suits that we would step in. We were so sharp in our black and gold satin suits. My mom tailor-made most of them so they were done right. When we finished pledging, Big D and Joe were right there for Carrie and me. The Alphas had a party in the Alpha house, and once again we danced through the night. We began to see each other every night after choir, and the love connection was on. We officially belonged to each other as a boyfriend/girlfriend kind of thing.

Summer came and we both went to summer school. Big D would come to my house, and my dad liked him and Mom seemed to like him, too. My brother, James, told me that all the boys from Memphis wanted from a Pine Bluff girl is what's between her legs. I laughed and told him he was just a brother who was over-protecting his sister. My brother James loved me and had taken special care of me all his life. He even said that some guys told him that Big D was gay because he dressed so good. I said to him, "You dress good so, what, are you gay, too?" I laughed and went on but he never smiled because he was serious.

The fall of 1975, everyone knew we were a couple so no one tried to cut in on Big D. I really enjoyed my classes and studied a lot. Big D and I spent a lot of evenings after choir together. I always carried my books and he rarely carried books. He would study mostly at night from 11:00 P.M. to 2:00 A.M. His mother would call him every morning from Memphis, Tennessee, and wake him up for his eight o'clock class. He was the only child she had, and he was spoiled.

I wanted to pledge Alpha Kappa Alpha (fall 1975) because my aunt and cousins were AKAs, plus people would tease me and say that since I looked half-white, I fit that sorority. The Alpha Kappa Alpha sorority had a rush, and I attended. Carrie wanted to pledge Delta because she thought red and white was wonderful, and she made several friends with the Delta Sigma Thetas.

I was selected to pledge, and we pledged six long weeks. We walked two by two or in a straight line all six weeks. We ran for exercise after dinner each night. That's the only time I remember weighing a hundred thirty-five pounds, and I felt cute. I was always on the heavy-set side. When Big Sisters realized that I was Big D's girlfriend, I was tortured every night. One Big Sister told me she was sleeping with him every night, but all I could say was, "Okay, Big Sister; Ivies don't have boyfriends." I would have to go through this each night. There was no way I could see him during pledging so the Big Sisters who were in choir would allow me to at least look around at him. I was so tired that I couldn't even think about a relationship. Our pledge show day came, and we wore dark-green and light-green satin jacket tops and skirts. My mom came through once again with the tailored outfits, but this time when a Big Sister once saw how well my suit was made, she gave it to another pledge. My heart was truly broken because my mother showed her love for me by making my clothes. The suit I wore was what my mother would have called botched-up. But the show went on, and all the Alpha Phi Alphas were there to see us, and we stepped as cute as AKAs do. I was excited especially about wearing make-up because I had never gotten into it. They made my face up, and I felt like another person. Truly, it was special. My hair was flipped and bouncin' and behavin'. Our line was named the Tantalizing Twenty. My line name was "Mother Dearest" because I was always taking care of somebody while we were pledging.

Pledging days had ended. I was a member of the Alpha Angel Society and Alpha Kappa Alpha sorority. I had made it up the college social ladder. I was involved and everyone knew me, and that was fine with me. Thanksgiving came, and semester exams were upon us. David (Big D's real name), as I began to call him, would go home for Christmas, and I too joined my family. When we returned, we seemed to be so tight, and more and more we would see each other after choir.

My birthday of 1976 was really special. David had a party at his house for me. People came and partied long and hard. Remember, he had broken up with Bernice and had taken his engagement ring back from her. He told me that he wanted to marry me and asked me if I would wear the engagement ring. I was so happy. He had had the ring cleaned, and it sparkled with a few diamonds and white gold. I thought for a minute, "I am wearing a hand-me-down ring but I guess it's okay: it's the thought that counts." We kissed and kissed. We returned to everyone else at the party and I showed off my ring. The next few days my hand was just a showpiece as word spread around about my birthday present. Even when we went to choir the next time Mr. McPhee told me to show everybody so the whispering in choir could stop. I felt so much in love. This was David's last semester in college, and I felt he was trying to secure his relationship with me before he left for graduate school. He always had a goal of furthering his education and talked about it often.

We mostly saw each other at choir. Choir tour time came, and we had a one-day trip to Arkadelphia, Arkansas. When we all got seated on the bus we talked, laughed, and sang all the way there. We had a wonderful concert, and the food afterward was really good. We then boarded the bus to return to campus. Again we talked, laughed, and sang on the bus. Near the middle of the trip the guys headed for the back of the bus. They were all telling about how many babies they each had, and I was too surprised at the very nature of the conversation. Well, David told them he had a little girl, and I thought I would faint. I got quiet and began to think. My parents always told me not to get involved with a person who is married or persons who had children out of wedlock. As I sat and thought, I said to myself, "This is over as soon as we reach campus." Just before we reached campus David returned to his seat and began trying to talk to me. I told him it was all over since he had a little girl. He told me over and over that he was just getting into the conversation and that having a baby was just a show of manhood. I told him to leave me alone and that I didn't believe him. I got off the bus and wouldn't allow him to walk me to the dorm. He was really trying to tell me he was just kidding around. When I reached the dorm I was so angry and felt betrayed. Later that night I got a phone call on my hall, and it was David's mother telling me that he didn't have any children and that he was only kidding and if he did have any she would spank him good. She said she had taught him to leave the girls alone and especially no babies. I felt she was telling the truth so I called him and told him his mother saved the relationship because I just don't play like that.

Our next choir tour was to St. Louis, and we went to the zoo and sang at churches where our college alumni attended. The people were so nice everywhere we sang. We had an excellent choir with an awesome sound.

Graduation Day came for David, all too quickly for me. His family attended the graduation, and I sang in the choir. It was hard to think that he wouldn't be in choir next year. People were hugging and crying all around with mixed feelings of joy and sadness. The next day when everyone was packing to leave, he decided to spend time with me. We talked about his being away and how we needed to be true to one another. The moments were so intense with love. He asked me to ride to Memphis with him to visit and meet again with his family because they had planned a graduation party for him and he wanted me to celebrate with him. I wasn't sure if my parents would allow me to go. I talked with my mom because my father was so strict and most of the time I was afraid to ask him anything. My mom told me it was okay and asked when I would be coming back. I told her I thought we would return on Sunday. Traveling to Memphis was always a special treat for me because I got to go across the large bridge that connected Arkansas and Tennessee. I still feel like it's the best river crossing in the country.

We talked as we always had and discussed what he planned to do. He had been accepted to the University of Northern Iowa to work on his master's in music education. He was so smart, but I still couldn't figure out why he wanted to go to such a cold place.

When we got to his parents' home, too much excitement was in the air. His family and friends were simply crazy about him. I greeted everyone and usually there was always his father, his mother, Papa Jack, Miss Driver, his cousin Lavonia, and her son T.J. I was generally quiet around the family because I didn't really know how to communicate with them so I felt it best to say as little as possible. Everything was always about David anyway, but it didn't bother me much because my family discussed me a lot, too.

We soon dressed and went to David's cousin Sonia Lyle's home. It was nice and decorated for the occasion. Lavonia rode over in the car with us, and we talked a lot. She was always easy to talk to, and she seemed to like me. As other family members gathered, the party was on. There were lots of foods, drinks, and people talking, drinking, and smoking what they shouldn't. It was a live party. For David's graduation gift I had purchased his college class ring. He was crazy about it, and it had his initials, his fraternity, and school symbols on it. It was a pretty classy gift. He showed his ring off to most of the party people. A cousin, Connie, whom the family affectionately calls Candi, asked me why I liked her cousin so much, and why did I buy him such a nice gift? She was so harsh that I went to the bathroom and began to cry. Lavonia found me crying and told me to not pay attention to Candi and that it was okay. When David found out I had been crying he told me to just stay near him. He seemed to always try and buffer me from certain members of his family. We stayed and talked to Cousin Sonia, and she was nice to me. She always liked David and me as a couple and felt we could make it. She never talked down to me. I was always fascinated with her because she was a very attractive woman who had things together. She could always entertain with stories about the family. We had been talking so long that it was 4:00 A.M. We told her thanks for the party and that we would try to visit before we left. It always seemed strange to me that whenever we visited in his parent's home we always came in around 4:00 A.M., and Thornton's donuts were always the snack on the way home. We eased into the house, and he slept on the couch while I slept in his bedroom. His parents were snoring so we both laughed and then kissed and hugged and headed for bed.

In the morning we awoke to the smell of bacon frying, steak, gravy, white rice, and Thornton's donuts. There was always lots and lots of food in the house, and Miss Driver and Susie were always cooking one thing or another. It was Saturday morning, and their day had begun. I lay in bed and listened to the movement in the home. The phone rang, and Susie told the person on the other end that if she came now she would meet her in the beauty shop to fix her hair. James was answering the knock at the door. James, David's dad, was what you call a loan shark, and people were coming to borrow money from him. James was a trucking supervisor for Time DC, and Susie was a beautician. Their home was located in the Orange Mound area of Memphis, the oldest black settlement in the country. It was prominent because blacks who lived here were buying their homes and worked good jobs since the slaves were liberated. All I knew was that it was a busy household with people coming in and out all the time. During the day it was never a quiet moment.

The door opened in the bedroom, and it was David. He lay across the bedspread and began to talk to me. He told me his mother was cooking for a bar-b-que this afternoon and had invited friends and relatives. I laughed to myself, "Another party." We soon finished talking and got up to get dressed. I made sure I made my bed up because my mom always taught me to make my bed and help around the house even when you are visiting someone. As the day progressed, people were coming and going and I sat and watched and heard many conversations. All of Susie's friends would come in and kiss David and hug him and say, "You see, this is my baby." Everybody loved David.

Susie had four miscarriages before she gave birth to David, and all her friends knew the hard times she had had and what she had been through. So when she finally gave birth to David, who she said weighed in at ten pounds, everybody in the family and friends saw him as an extra-special blessing. That explained why everybody was so glad to see him. Music was playing, and the bar-b-que smoker was going, the picnic table was set; Cokes and all kinds of drinks were in the cooler. I sat and I watched as people ate, played cards, carried plates home, talked, and told jokes. The backyard was full. I thought the family was having a neighborhood party. People were everywhere.

We soon slipped away and went to Overton Square. This was a place where you could walk around in shops, hear music, and see several restaurants. We went to a disco club and danced the night away. Coming in again at 4:00 A.M., we repeated our

Friday night routine. Once again early Sunday morning I woke to bacon frying, steak and gravy, white rice, and Thornton's donuts. The breakfast table was full of food. Sunday morning people began knocking on the door for James to borrow money. We began to get ready for church. I had been awake a long time because I was used to going to Sunday School on Sundays at 9:30 A.M. We were still in bed at that time. It felt so strange to me missing Sunday School but I relieved myself by saying, "You're visiting and you're out of town so it's okay." By the time we ate, got dressed, and out to church it was 11:30.

I couldn't believe we arrived at church so late. David's home church was Middle Baptist Church located on Lamar Avenue with the Reverend Franklin Jones as pastor. He was also well known for his active role in the NAACP as well as the civil rights movement. He was a dynamic preacher. We found our seat and sat down. The choir was singing, and the spirit was high. The sisters were dressed in beautiful hats, and the clothes were too tough. Susie fit right in. She always dressed fashionably and wore shoes to match everything. David always dressed sharp, too. I couldn't begin to tell you what I had on because clothes have never been high on my list of priorities; however, I'm sure I looked neat in whatever I had on. When the church secretary asked for visitors to stand, I stood up and smiled. I was thanked for coming to visit and took my seat. When Reverend Jones realized David was in the congregation he asked him to come up and render a solo. While he was coming he talked about how he had baptized him as a young boy and how he was so proud that he had completed his college degree. David sang "His Eye is on the Sparrow," and everyone's heart was touched. After a most moving sermon I got to shake the hand of the famous Franklin Jones, and then I sat in the pew as I watched David talk to several of the members. They hugged and kissed him and were so glad to see him.

When we returned home from church Papa Jack, David's grandfather, was sitting on the porch. He always smiled at me and said, "You're such a nice girl." We went into the house and prepared ourselves for the journey back to Arkansas. After eating Sunday dinner and talking to Lavonia and playing with T.J. we got into the car and headed back to Arkansas.

The summer after his graduation (1976) he worked at Sears. I was attending summer school and was living at home with my parents. He would come over and talk to my family and visit with whoever was around at the time. My parents owned a grocery store so we were always busy. Most of our conversation that summer was about missing and being away from one another. We certainly dreaded the day being separated. While visiting me one summer evening, David asked my mother if he could marry me. My mother told him if he could leave and go away to school and take care of his educational goals while I finished my own she would allow him to return and marry me. Then she said, "It's up to Deborah though whether you're who she wants to marry." He tried to tell her I could finish college by transferring with him and she said, "No, it is a family tradition to graduate from the University of Arkansas at Pine Bluff." He seemed disappointed, but I knew he wouldn't dare ask my dad because anyone who dated me was afraid of my father. We walked out and sat on the front steps and talked quietly. In my mind I was glad my mom had said what she did. I wanted to finish college, and I had promised my parents that I would get married only after college was completed, and I didn't want to break my promise. I never told David this.

The moving day finally came. His father came and packed up everything into the truck. We talked and said we would call each other. We said that we would talk every Thursday night at 11:00 P.M.

David moved to Cedar Falls, Iowa, with a full scholarship in music education. He told me he was living in the graduate housing and his room was very nice.

I lived with my parents that summer to the very last day. I knew it would be hard to face campus without David being there. No more fun in choir and no more getting picked up late. In short, I was not looking forward to going back to school. I knew I had to go so I could meet my goal, knowing I would be the third child of my parents to graduate college, and I wanted to carry the legacy on. My dad and mom took me to the campus and helped me get things into my room. I tried to greet my old friends with excitement but it was hard to smile while David was missing from the picture. I managed to not have a roommate my senior year, and it was great. I was able to keep my mind on my studies. I kept a tight schedule to make sure I stayed busy so as to not miss David so much.

I registered for eighteen hours the first semester and nineteen hours the second semester. In addition to that, I cleaned professors' homes and sat with a doctor's wife recovering from a heart attack. My weekends were spent with three precious little girls, my nieces whom I loved to spend time with. I kept this routine up, and when I looked around it was college homecoming day. David had been calling every Thursday as he promised, and we talked about when he was coming to town. I could live on just knowing he would be coming back soon. He arrived and stayed with some old fraternity brothers. We attended the homecoming parade and game together and went to the Alpha Phi Alpha fraternity house that night. It was so late when he walked me back to the dorm, and I just wanted to keep walking forever as long as I was with him. He flew out on Sunday and it was back to the same old busy schedule, but this time I had Christmas holidays to look forward to.

Between homecoming and Christmas my old boyfriend, Daniel Davis, began to call me at the dorm. He told me that he heard I was engaged and that he loved me and didn't want me to marry David. He begged me to go out with him. My girlfriend Marcia was short and sassy, and she had a mouth that wouldn't quit. I saw her coming down the hallway and I motioned to her to come near me. While Daniel was on the phone talking and begging to see me I told Marcia I was going to see him and that I wanted her to go with me. She knew David and she knew I loved him and she also knew that I had caught Daniel with another girl and that's why we had broken up. I got back to Daniel, and I told him that I would meet him in front of the college library at 9:00 P.M. He seemed so happy.

When I loved Daniel, I really loved him. He was what people called a high-yellow Negro, but he was on the heavy side. He had not finished college and was a radio DJ in town. He was twenty-two years old and still living at home with his parents. I had fallen out of love with him, and his not finishing school did not help at all. I was looking for a man going somewhere, and David was at least in graduate school.

Marcia and I began to get ready to make the 9:00 P.M. meeting. Before David left he had given me a shirt that said on the front "PROPERTY OF DAVID." I put that shirt on, and Marcia just screamed. After laughing and putting our shoes on, we left the dorm and walked across the parking lot to the library. Daniel thought I was coming alone, but I had Marcia to come with me because if I couldn't help him understand the message that I was engaged, I knew she had my back. When we turned the corner on the parking lot, there Daniel sat in his long Cadillac. I thought that maybe when I saw him I would get that love flutter. You know, the flutter you get when you see someone you truly love. Honey, there was no flutter, no bells, no whistles, nor lights, and that let me know for sure I was over him and that my heart had been assigned to another. I spoke to him and asked him how he had been doing. He said he missed me and I said, "Well you've seen me," while making sure I didn't cross my arms to cover up the writing on my shirt. He soon noticed and said, "Is that all he left you?" and I said, "No," and showed him my ring. He told me over and over he was sorry about the reason we broke up, but I said it was over and I kept telling him that over and over. Marcia was standing quietly by my side. Daniel asked who she was and why she'd come with me. Marcia quickly said, "I'm her bodyguard, and you have used up enough of her time." She began to work that mouth and told him that he was a loser and it was over and to get lost. We walked away and I never saw Daniel any more that year. We went back to the dorm and laughed and talked about the look of losing he had on his face. Marcia returned to her room and I turned to my favorite late night show, *Perry Mason*, which is the only show I had time to watch.

My college classes were going well, and I studied a lot. David continued to call me on Thursdays at 11:00 P.M. I always looked forward to Thursdays on the phone with David. Christmas was fast approaching. It was college finals and then coming home for the holidays. David flew home to Memphis, and he would call me each night.

He came to visit and spent one night with us. My mom made me sleep in the bed with her while he slept upstairs in my bedroom. When morning came I went upstairs and told him that he needed to get dressed because breakfast would be served soon. He reminded me that he did not eat breakfast. I told him if he was seriously planning to get into this family he would have to learn to eat breakfast. Mom had prepared bacon, eggs, sausage, rice, waffles, and coffee for Daddy. We talked about the difference between his family's breakfast and my family's breakfast and laughed. Soon Mom was calling us to come downstairs and eat breakfast. We came quickly because Dad did not like waiting to eat. He would always pray quickly, and everyone else said a Bible verse from memory. Even what he prayed was from memory. After prayer we began to eat, but as the food was being passed around I could tell David was having a hard time making a selection. He put rice on his plate because his mom ate rice each morning. When the waffles came around he took one and then, instead of pancake syrup, he asked for jelly. My dad said quickly, "You don't like syrup?" and he said, "I really don't eat breakfast foods." He told my dad his mom always fixed steak, chicken, gizzards, rice, and gravy at breakfast. My mom and I just sat quietly.

Breakfast was over soon, and we cleaned the kitchen and finished the dishes.

Thoughts of the wedding were in the air, and we talked about exactly what we wanted for the wedding. Mom explained to David that we needed to select a china pattern for our dishes, and then we talked about the rehearsal dinner and the menu for it. My mom, David, and I made all the plans for the wedding. We started very early. Mom had some errands to run so we decided to go with her. We stopped at Kahn's Jewelers, and they were having a sale. Mom sat and talked to the sales clerk while we shopped for our wedding rings. The prices varied so much, and at that time I didn't know or understand carat weights and diamond size. I was only looking at the sales price. We found a beautiful trio for about two hundred dollars. It had a quarter-carat-weight diamond with fine cuts in the gold band for a design effect. The shine was totally awesome, and we were smiling from ear to ear. We decided to purchase them, and we agreed to put them on layaway and we would pay equal amounts each month until they were paid off. I still wore the last girlfriend's ring until we exchanged vows.

When we finished our ring business we told Mom what we had done, and she was pleased. She began to talk again about the china pattern so we looked at dishes, bowls, glasses, etc. When David saw the prices he asked my mom, "Can't we just buy paper plates?" He was under the impression that we were purchasing all our fine china. We laughed, and Mom and I could tell he did not understand the process. When she told him people would give us each piece, there was a sense of relief on his face. Once he understood that, he began to choose the finest and the best china. I said to him, "We should get dishes that we could use every day instead of sitting up in a showcase." We found a pattern that had a band of dark green on the edge and a cluster of fruit in the center. It was Cornwall wear, and its plates came at a price of eight dollars per plate. Mom suggested we have an eight-piece setting. We also selected water goblets and ice cream goblets. Our place settings were gold-plated. I was used to silverware so this was very unique to me. Mom was pleased with our choices and so was Mrs. Kahn, the store owner. We left the store, and Mom had to show David the monkey I wanted for Christmas as a little girl in the Otasco store. She told David that when I was three years old, I begged for a monkey for Christmas, but when we came to the store to see it, I cried with fright. David laughed and teased me about the monkey.

We returned home and began to prepare lunch. Daddy bar-b-qued so we had ribs, chicken, and beef. His bar-b-que was the best. He would smoke it from 4:00 A.M. to 9:00 P.M. And the meat would fall off the bone. The flavor was down to the bone and made you want to eat the bone. It's no other taste than that of my Dad's bar-b-que. Lunch was on the table, and we sat down to eat. We ate so much that we lost track of how many chickens or how many ribs we ate. After dinner Dad and David went to the store while Mom and I cleaned up the kitchen. I came from a truly traditional family where the men ate and left for outside work and women stayed in the home cooking, sewing, and cleaning. Many girls today do not have the above-mentioned skills. It was a way of life for us then with no known options.

David returned from talking to Dad in the store and we sat in the den and watched TV. At one point I sat on his lap and my mom saw me. She called me to her room and said, "It's not nice for ladies to sit on the lap of a young man." I knew what she meant so when I returned to the den I sat on my own chair as Mom had instructed.

The phone rang, and my mom called David to the phone. It was his mom calling to say that someone had passed away in his family and he needed to come to Memphis right away. I helped him gather his things. I told him to call me later, and he promised he would. After he left I went and picked up my nieces (my brother's daughters) because they were always a favorite to help me pass the time away. Those little girls were the sweetest, most precious things on earth to me. I always liked to dress them up and comb their hair. If their hair got out of place I would comb it again.

I would sit and talk with Mom but not too often because she was always sewing our clothes. (After reading the Bible story about Dorcus I began to call my mom Dorcus in adulthood because she made clothes for everyone.)

My father's mom, Grandmother Cassie, was sweet with age and wisdom. She always watched soap operas and lived next door to us. You knew not to visit her from 11:00 A.M. to 3:00 P.M. because she would only talk to you during commercial breaks. She could tell you years and years of the people and their soap opera lives. Grandmother Cassie would dip snuff and kept a Maxwell House coffee can to spit in. I thought it was the most grotesque thing I'd ever seen. She was such a good listener and when you finished talking, she always imparted words of wisdom. I remember one time Daddy made me so mad I told her he was not right and he was unfair and she would answer, "He is still your daddy, no matter what; he is still your daddy." Another time she told me how she was a midwife and that she delivered eighteen children and breastfed them all. I thought, "This woman has to be made of steel," but the wrinkles in her face and silver in her hair was not a hard look, but a graceful one. You could tell she knew how to survive and was all of ninety-two years old. She often experienced pains from her gallbladder, and I would sit with her through the pain while her children were frightened that she was always taking her last breath. I knew she would be all right and that it was just another spell she was having.

When I sat with her I would often tell her she ought to stop scaring them like that, and for a moment we would both laugh. During her pain I would hear her say, "My Lord, Lord, help." She was a preacher's wife so I knew she had a fear of God and loved Him as well because, though she never said it, I know she had to trust a mighty God to bring her through relationships, chores, midwifery, and eighteen children. To me, she was strong to out-last all her friends and relatives. Her monthly social security check gave her about $1.01 a month for each year she had lived. She smiled, and the silver shined in her hair. When I told her I was getting married, she was quite happy. She liked David and when he would visit she always liked him to talk to her. Her advice to me in our private time was, "Do not start anything in your marriage you cannot keep up with." I really had to sit and think about why Grandmother said that, but once married it all fell into place. Those moments and times visiting Grandmother will always be special in my heart.

Christmas came with all of its traditions and we were always prepared for it. My mom shopped a year in advance so we always looked forward most to the day after Christmas to make the after-Christmas sales. We would shop for fabrics and other things like bows, wrapping paper, and Christmas name tags. This is still a tradition for me today. Mom was a very thrifty person—and talk about recycling: she could make something out of nothing. The rest of my Christmas break from college was spent with Mom and Dad, my brother Matthew, and my nieces.

The day came, and Dad returned me to the campus. I would always have Dad to drop me off because if my nieces saw me leave, they would cry after me. David had called often and told me that he had really enjoyed the visit and he too had returned to school. He was in his second semester of graduate school and I was in second semester of my senior year. Returning to register, I wanted to graduate in August 1977 so I knew my work was cut out for me. I couldn't believe it, but my grades were such that they allowed me to take seven classes, which translates into nineteen hours. This was very good for me because that semester flew by so fast. Between classes, studying, running home on the weekend, and Thursday night 11:00 P.M. talks with David, time was moving. I was majoring in Institutional Dietetics, and the one class out of the seven that I struggled with that semester was Experimental Foods. My professor for that class was young, and there were only six of us in the class. She was a new graduate from Purdue University and she taught on a Ph.D. level to us. Dr. Hurst was too much. She could never repeat a statement twice, and her exams killed you every time she gave one. No matter how much I read and studied, I never could make a decent grade on her exams. She was too tough. I was so stressed by her class at one point that my mom sensed the stress and told me she was going to call Dr. Virginia Meriwether, the department head, and speak to her about this professor. I assured her that I would be okay. After struggling all semester it was finals time. I had all As in my other classes, but when Dr. Hurst posted her grades I had a D. The other students' grades listed with mine were one C, my D, three Fs, and one incomplete. I thanked God over and over for that D. I was never so glad and happy to see a D in all my life. I just needed to pass. I had nightmares that I would not pass and I couldn't get married as we planned. The D in my sight was real good. I had passed, and I could get away from stressful Dr. Hurst's class. Thank God. After carrying nineteen hours (seven classes) with all As, that D was okay for me. Bottom line: the course was behind me, over and out.

That summer, David and I both were attending summer school and I was once again, for the last summer, at home. This summer was really interesting. My mother's mom came to live with us for about six weeks. Grandmother Julia was a beautiful high-yellow-skinned person. She was not always in her right mind and was in an arthritic state. Her knees could not bend, and she was unable to walk. Her hands were deformed by the arthritic condition, but she was able to feed herself. She was a character. She would not eat leftover food and on top of that was very particular about what she ate. She would stress my mom out all day just calling "Clidis" (Claudia). When I would return home in the afternoon from summer school I would tell her,

"Grandma Julia, don't call Mom. I'm here and I'll help you." She would get so quiet because she knew she couldn't get away with keeping up that noise with me at home. At night I slept at the end of the bed, and when she needed to go to the bathroom I would get up and help her. Sometimes she would wake me four times during the night. Even though I was taking classes I felt I could handle the stress better than my mom having her all day and all night. My mom was so appreciative, and I know she was able to rest well at night. I would study in the evening before helping Grandma Julia to bed and then sometimes in the mornings. Grandma Julia could be a handful at times. By the time her six weeks were up, we were glad that she was going to Aunt Frankie's house, my mother's sister. The timing was good because I had to spend my last four weeks of summer school in a dietetic undergraduate intern program. I traveled to Little Rock, Arkansas, and applied as a manager of the camp cafeteria for Camp Ferndale, which is a United Methodist summer camp for children of various ages. I interviewed with Mr. Samford and was hired on the spot. I had no experience other than what I had learned in college and working in the family grocery store growing up. As the new cafeteria manager I planned menus, ordered foods, prepared the meals, and cleaned up.

A private cabin was provided for me in the woods just off from the kitchen. I had no fear of being by myself in the woods. The campus was beautiful, and during slow times I would participate in the activities of the camp. David would still continue to call me on Thursdays at 11:00 P.M. That was our special date at night away from one another. I hired a cook my second week at the camp. She was an older lady and, boy, was she ever set in her ways. One evening I had placed cornbread on the menu, and she refused to cook it. It had been requested. I decided I would try to make it. Being college-trained and family-trained to cook by my mom and two aunts, I knew my cornbread would be all right. After mixing the cornbread and baking it, it had the appearance of being a prize-winning bread; however, when

I went to cut it into pieces it was so tough. The whole pan was like rubber. I cut it and served it to the kids anyway. To see the look on their faces trying to bite that rubber cornbread was too funny. Mr. Samford said after that experience, and not to hurt my feelings, "Kids don't like to eat cornbread away from home much anyway so let's just stick to the purchased rolls." I laughed and called my mom to tell her what had happened. Of course, you know she told me what went wrong with the bread. Cornbread at camp was never mentioned again.

We always worked eight days on and four days off at camp so my mom would pick me up. We always talked about the wedding plans, and things were moving right along. When I would arrive home I would remember to make payments on our rings, and I didn't want to forget that. I wanted yellow and green as the wedding colors. My mom volunteered to make all the bridesmaids' dresses, flower girl dress, her own dress, and dresses for my nieces. She put together my veil, but I told her a wedding gown would be just too much and that she would be too tired at the wedding. I never asked her if she felt hurt not making my wedding dress. She was then and even now a very capable seamstress. We looked for patterns, fabrics, lace, and the like. We were always busy on my visits from camp.

David completed his master's degree in music education and graduated that summer. I was unable to attend the graduation due to my own commitments. David returned to Memphis from Cedar Falls, and he soon came to visit me at Camp Ferndale. He was afraid of the dark, but everyone assured him that he would enjoy his one-night stay. He returned to Memphis with a list of things to do for the wedding. The guys were wearing white tuxedos with yellow/green cummerbunds. He had to order them and bring them in from Memphis. He had his assignments, and I just asked that he follow through. We had selected our bridesmaids, maid of honor, best man, and groomsmen from among our closest friends and family members. The last camp finally ended, and I cleaned that little camp kitchen

up for the last time. That evening the other staff gave me a
bridal shower, and we had so much fun. The next day Mom
picked me up and also picked up my only sister, Reetta, up from
the airport. I had only seven days to get everything tight and in
place for the wedding.

Monday morning, my sister and I got up early on a mission
going to find a wedding dress. As we were driving, she told me
she was the older sister and I was supposed to wait until she
got married first. I told her my man was waiting, and I said,
"I'm sorry but the wedding is on." We laughed and talked as we
headed for Jefferson Square. This was the latest strip shopping
center that had stores in an L shape. We stopped at New Maru
that used to be a local downtown store. It was a high-class store
that had moved to the strip shopping center. We went in and I
began to search the sale rack. I didn't want to spend a lot for
the dress because I knew I would only be in it for a short period
of time. I tried on size twelve after size twelve dress and then I
found the one I wanted. My dress fit so well, and it was on sale
for a hundred fifty dollars. My mom made the wedding veil to
match my dress. The dress I chose had a fitted midriff with lace
and pearl. It had a high neckline with lace from the waist to the
floor; it was full and beautiful with lace and pearls throughout.
A not-so-long train was part of the dress. The sleeves were long
and sheer and had ruffles at the wrist. My veil was of long net-
ting, and the head piece was covered with floral lace and satin.
I decided to get the dress so I paid for it and the lady put it in
a nice long white bag. Have you ever heard of someone getting
their wedding gown six days prior to the big wedding day? Yes,
that's me; I am not hard to please. We put the dress in the car,
relieved that we completed our one mission. We started looking
for white pumps. During my last day of camp I had dropped
a trash can on my right big toe, and the closed-toe shoe was
killing my toe. When I found a pair of shoes that didn't hurt
as much as the rest, I paid for them and we were off. I never
thought about wearing a dressy sandal. I guess I was trying to

keep up that tradition of wearing dress pumps with the wedding gown.

The week of the wedding was truly busy. I talked to David every night. The doorbell was ringing often with wedding gifts being delivered from the jewelry store. There were round boxes, square boxes, colorfully wrapped boxes, and they were all being opened and logged in the bridal gift registry. Everything coming in was very useful. I had never seen so many gifts in one place. People were truly generous, and God was blessing us before we had even begun our venture of married life. Mom was wrapping up all the little last-minute dress alterations, reception plans, and floral arrangements. My mom and I did a super job of planning the wedding. Just weeks before, David and I had attended marriage counseling with the Reverend Jeffery Hickson, Sr. He talked about marriage and related the Scriptures to the marriage. I am sure that I was so in love that a lot of the counseling was just formality. I remember he asked David if he was Baptist and if he had been in church all of his life, and he answered "yes." Then he asked him if I was the only woman of all the other women in the world that he wanted to spend his entire life with, and he said "yes." I felt so special when he gave that answer. He asked me the same questions, and I answered "yes." He explained to us how to get the marriage license, and our counseling session ended.

All week gifts were pouring in, and my dad was the only real person with real thoughts in the house. He would ask me daily, "What's the nigger gon' do?" That meant he wanted to know what kind of job David had. He told me, "No job, no wedding, and I don't care how much preparing you have done." He was plain and simply serious. He had lived long enough to know that love couldn't pay anybody's bills. I was so afraid of my daddy, and he always said what he meant and he meant what he said. So I called David and told him that if we were going to be married on Saturday he needed to get a job even if it was just pumping gas. I explained to him what my daddy had said, and he knew he better get job hunting fast. By the next evening when we talked he told me he had a temporary teaching job for one semester at a school in Waterloo, Iowa, and that he would have to report to work first thing Monday morning. No late excuses accepted. You had to be there and be there on time. You better believe I was so happy to give my dad the news about the job so I could relax and give him relief also. I guess it's every father's job is to protect their little girls to the very last moment before they give them to another man. My dad was just that kind. He seemed to pride himself in screening my boyfriends. Just the same he was watching out for me because I was soaked in love and the beauty of the frills and the event itself that I couldn't see past all that.

Relatives began to arrive from out of town that Thursday, and the house was full of people and we were eating and talking and answering the door for gifts. My little nieces seemed to sense the festivities and they were clinging to me seemingly more than ever. Those three little girls were so near and dear to me! I loved them so much, and I learned so much from them during the short time of our lives together before I was to get married and leave home. Venus, my oldest niece, was my flower girl and she was just the right age, simply precious.

On Friday we knew it would be more of the same but I was excited because David was already in town, and the rehearsal and rehearsal dinner were at 6:00 P.M. on Friday evening. Nicole, my second niece, was turning four so we had a birthday celebration for her. We always loved to celebrate their birthdays. When David arrived, he greeted everyone in the house. We didn't stand around and talk much because we had to go to the courthouse and pick up our marriage license. We soon left for the courthouse, and it was good to get away from all the hustle and bustle for a moment.

While waiting for our marriage license at the courthouse it was announced over the radio that Elvis Presley had died (8/18/77). David was supposed to secure a hotel room in

Memphis for the night after the wedding. We knew that with this kind of news everyone in the world would be in Memphis for his funeral. We called David's mother while waiting for our license. David's mother, Susie, was best friends with Marcy, Elvis Presley's cook, and Marcy had asked Susie to come and help her at the Presley mansion for a few days. Susie told us that people were all over Memphis and there were no hotel rooms. Susie had a friend named Anna who had a nice small cottage-type house, and she told us they would fix it up for our honeymoon house. We told her that would be nice.

The lady finally called our names to pick up our license. We paid five dollars each for a total of ten dollars for our marriage license. We hugged and kissed and we were on our way to the church office to give the license to Reverend Hickson. When we arrived David asked him if he could read a poem to me at the wedding. He asked to see the poem. You see, when Reverend Hickson saw David this time he wasn't quite sure about him. His mother had put a perm in his hair and it was straight, so his appearance was totally different from when he met David the first time. When he saw the poem was good and written with genuine love, he did approve it to be read at the wedding. We left the visit with the minister knowing that truly by Saturday we would have all our ducks in a row, leaving no stone unturned.

As we came in the house, more relatives were there and more gifts had arrived. We ate dinner and I went to bed completely exhausted. Friday morning came and I was totally excited. The rehearsal and rehearsal dinner was at 6:00 P.M. As we were busy during the day with odds and ends, we were wrapping things up quickly. At the rehearsal everyone took their places and Venus, my oldest niece, was the flower girl, and Keith, a little boy I baby-sat, was the ring bearer. They were both five years old and just cute as they could be. Everyone knew that they would be the talk of the wedding.

After the rehearsal we went to the fellowship hall of the

church where we had a menu of my dad's famous bar-b-que ribs, chicken, and beef. We had coleslaw, corn on the cob, baked beans, light bread, assorted drinks, and cake. We fed a room filled with relatives and friends. David played the piano and sang during dinner. After dinner I presented gifts to our parents, bridesmaids, maid of honor, best man, groomsmen, and others who had helped us with the wedding. We really had a great evening, and everyone had fun. When I arrived at home I was so tired I could hardly see straight. My aunts, David's cousin Lavonia, who was a bridesmaid in the wedding, and her son, T.J., spent the night with us. My mom told me to sleep in the bed with her. She talked all night as I drifted in and out of sleep. She was excited too because she had worked so hard for months and finally the big day was upon us: the night before the wedding.

I got up real early that Saturday morning. I had a hair appointment with Mrs. Matthews, who had been fixing my hair since I was five years old. While Mrs. Matthews washed my hair we talked the old times and all the good times. She was taking extra special care of me that morning. My hair was simply beautiful when she had finished. I told her thanks and that whenever I would come home to visit she would still have to make room for me, and she promised she would. I felt so good because I knew with my hair done that it wasn't much left to do. Mom had fixed a light lunch so we packed the car and headed for Aunt Cassa's house. Aunt Cassa was mom's first cousin and our second, but because of age difference we always called her Aunt Cassa. She lived right next door to the church, and this is where we got dressed for the wedding. The guys dressed at the church in the classrooms. While waiting to get dressed I remembered David needed to have my rings so I sent them over to him by Lillie Bankhead, a family friend, whose sister Lenora was in my wedding. She took the rings over and came back so fast I asked her, "Did you see him? Was he really the one you gave the rings to?" I couldn't believe it. I told all the bridesmaids he was serious about marrying me because he was on time for once in his life. Mom and Aunt Cassa helped me dress, and soon I was standing there before the mirror looking simply beautiful. My heart was pounding, and I was just nervous. I paused for a moment and thanked God for helping me thus far. Word came from the groomsmen that one groomsman had not arrived so we waited about twenty minutes after 2:00 P.M. David's half-brother had gotten lost coming from Memphis to Pine Bluff for the wedding. David looked in to the audience and got Carl August, one of his fraternity brothers, to step in for his half-brother. Soon word was sent that everything was ready to begin. What seemed such a short walk from Aunt Cassa's house to the church seemed to take forever.

When we arrived inside and each bridesmaid and groomsman came in, I knew my time was drawing near to appear. My mom had told us earlier that it probably wouldn't be a lot of people at the wedding since the date we had chosen was so close to school starting and people would use their Saturday to shop. When the wedding march began to play, Aunt Cassa motioned for me to step forward. My dad had his left arm locked into my right arm ready to walk me down the aisle. When I stepped to the center aisle at the back of the church all eyes were on me; I looked and the church was packed full of people. I then looked at David and I could tell we were truly in love and we both smiled so hard that I know all of both sets of our teeth were showing. At that moment it was as if no one else was there but us. Suddenly my dad broke the smiling trance by saying, "You don't have to go down there because no one will ever be able to take care of you like I have." I said, "Let's walk, and we will walk slowly." I heard what he said but I couldn't understand why he was saying it then and I thought, "He is still my protective father." After we walked down the aisle slowly, the wedding ceremony began. Reverend Hickson was dressed in his best robe, and he asked who was to give me away and my father said, "I do," and took his place next to Mom. David and I were finally together, and we were squeezing each other's hand. Reverend Hickson began the vows, and we both had to listen well so we could repeat them exactly as he said them to us; no one stumbled. My maid of honor and sister, Reetta, was saying on my left side, "Girl, there is a fly on your veil." Mr. McPhee, our college choir director, was singing "The Lord's Prayer" and the three of us were so tickled. It was just a lot going on after the vows.

When he pronounced us man and wife, we kissed a little, trying not to embarrass ourselves. We walked slowly back up the aisle smiling at everyone who had come to see us tie the knot. Then we circled around and came back to the front for the long picture-taking session. All I could think about now was that my toe was killing me and I had to take my foot out of that closed-toe shoe. What a relief. We took all of the traditional poses. Billy Flowers was the best photographer in town, and he did an excellent job for us; our pictures were super. Finishing the pictures in the sanctuary, we kissed and hugged so many of our friends who were waiting to see us. We hurried to the reception where the fellowship hall was filled with people waiting for a bite of cake and a sip of punch on that beautiful warm summer day. I only got a bite of cake when we took the picture. I had to wait a full year for another piece of cake. My toe continued to hurt so I removed the shoe and carried it around in my hand after most of the guests left. My mom said, "Deborah, is it hurting that bad?" I said, "Oh yes; it had began to throb." The photographer needed one more picture, one of David removing the garter belt from my leg.

We moved quickly to our places to change clothes. We returned to my parents' home and I picked up my suitcases ready to travel to Iowa by way of Memphis, Tennessee. We had several friends who came from Memphis so there was a large caravan. I remember hugging my parents goodbye on the front steps and then turning to wave goodbye once we were inside the 1967 Red Chevrolet Impala that David's dad bought for him when he began student teaching his last semester of college. When we turned left onto Highway 79 North, I looked back and waved one last time. I was thinking leaving Pine Bluff would never come, but in a split moment I was leaving never to return that same Deborah Felecia Williams. I wept a little inside about leaving home and especially those three precious little nieces of mine. I knew I would miss them the most because they had absorbed so much of my time that last year of college and before. They were not at the house when I left because I knew it would be too much for them to see me go and too much for me to leave them. They went home with their mom, who was my sister-in-law and a bridesmaid in the wedding. My brother James, her husband, did not attend the wedding. He and I had a special relationship. He was truly a big brother and protected me. I remembered when I told him David was my boyfriend and that he was from Memphis and the comments he made about what David wanted from me. He loved me a lot and really I don't think he wanted me to date or marry. When I told him that we were engaged to be married, he told me that David was gay. I told him that just because he liked to dress nice and wear nice clothes that people placed the gay assumption on him. He said one of his friends told him that. Besides, I thought gay people looked a certain way and talked a certain way and swished a certain way; I never really knew a true gay person. He never mentioned it again, and it never came to be in another conversation. I never gave it any thought. It was spoken and that's that. I am still unsure to this day why my brother didn't come to my wedding. Maybe he knew something for real that I wasn't able to accept or believe.

We were being chauffeured by Christopher Scott, who was a groomsman in the wedding. Chris, as we called him, was from Waterloo, Iowa, and was a good friend of David from his days at the University of Northern Iowa. I had heard David talk about him a lot. He was originally from Texas and from a large family. We mostly talked in the car about the wedding and some of the funny things that happened. David kept telling me in a whisper, "I am going to get you tonight," while we were taking pictures and we both would smile and laugh real big. I would answer, "Okay, okay. Just wait until tonight." Even in the car he was whispering, "You are all mine," and we talked, kissed, and snuggled all the way to Memphis. When we got to the Arkansas/Tennessee Bridge leading into Tennessee, I looked back once again with my heart focusing on home just one more time. The view of Memphis coming across the bridge was always such an awesome view. I would just get too excited. Only a person coming from and growing up in a small place would understand how I felt each time I crossed that bridge.

The traffic was heavy due to people in town for Elvis Presley's funeral. We arrived at Anna's home just a little after dark. Her home was a little dollhouse-type cottage, where we went to spend the night. There were several cars that drove up behind us and our friends Jason and Susan Cole (Susan was pregnant with their first child) were behind us also. Everyone began to get out of the cars and stretch after the two-hour drive. David and I walked to the door, and Anna opened the door and just screamed congratulations with a big smile on her face. She was so excited we had arrived. She said she had been getting ready for us for days. The house was just simply picture-perfect. Every room had candles in it and was clean, neat, and in order. It was truly a wedding cottage. As we entered the kitchen to view all that was in the refrigerator, we met Anna's boyfriend, who was drunk as he could be. He spoke and continued his drinking. We began to tell Anna how nice everything was and how much we really appreciated all her hard work to help us have a place to sleep for our first night of marriage. She said, "I have always loved David and his mother Susie and it's nothing I wouldn't do for them." As Chris began to bring our luggage into the house, Anna's drunken boyfriend began to question why was he bringing suitcases into the house. Anna told him that we were spending the night and he made no comment. After visiting with her for a bit longer she began to get her purse and tell her boyfriend that it was time to leave so they could sleep at his house tonight. He began cursing and saying he wasn't going no-damned-where and talked louder and louder, even getting a little combative. When we realized he was not going to calm down and leave, Jason and Susan offered to let us spend the night with them. They had just purchased their first home, and it was pretty. As with most new couples they said they had no extra bed and not much furniture, so we told them we would stay the night with them. Anna was so upset but we let her know that it was okay. She kept saying Susie would be terribly mad at her but we said we would explain. Our other friends had already wished us well and told us they would see us at my in-laws home before we left Memphis. Chris spent the night with my in-laws. We put our luggage back into Jason and Susan's car and we went home with them. Their home was so nice and quiet and sparsely furnished with furniture. Susan, being pregnant, was truly tired from the day's events, and I was whipped also. She fixed a little something to eat and we all sat and talked. We soon went to bed. We put blankets on the floor of one of their three bedrooms and slept there for the night. We were too tired to consummate the marriage; we hugged and kissed and we were soon both asleep.

Morning came and we realized we had escaped all the family and the other friends for one night. We awoke running and rushing to get to church. David's parents had planned a wedding reception after church so our friends in Memphis who couldn't travel to Pine Bluff would be able to see us and share our special time. Jason and David were slowing around while Susan and I waited and talked about first one thing and then another. When we finally arrived at church it was just letting out. People were in the fellowship hall of the church waiting for us. We were met with hugs, kisses, and lots of people saying congratulations. My mother-in-law was quite upset because David's eyes were red and he smelled like marijuana. She was really angry at him. Jason and David were dope-smoking partners in high school, and David had smoked all through college and was even arrested in college and busted for trying to sell weed. He always had respect for me and would not smoke in my presence too often. He never tried to influence me to be a partaker in his habit. I thought this was a trend and as soon as we got away from the environment he would stop smoking. My parents had come from Arkansas and had brought more gifts with them. We had several gifts at the reception. The table was laced with much food, and people were eating a lot. We talked to several people and thanked them for coming and being so generous to us. We left the reception and headed for my in–laws' house.

When we arrived, several family members were waiting to see us. My father-in-law James had rented a small U-Haul trailer for us to put our little furniture and gifts in. We filled that little trailer up. It was just the beginning. We knew we were on a time-line because David had to be at work on Monday morning at 8:00 A.M. Yes, his real job. People were coming from everywhere, it seemed, to tell us bye. Papa Jack, David's grandfather, told David to be good to me because I looked and seemed like a good girl. He was always on the porch to tell us goodbye whenever we came or left Memphis, and this time was no different. He was in the large number of well-wishers too. We pulled away from the house with Chris driving. We decided to split the driving up into four stretches. He drove first, David drove second, I drove third, and then Chris took us on to Cedar Falls. I didn't sleep much because I had traveled a lot as a child and I was accustomed to helping the driver stay awake. David was nodding so much when it was his turn to drive that I drove his time and mine too. It was okay because I was used to the road since a little girl. We arrived in Cedar Falls at 6:00 A.M. at the home of Dr. Larry and Jenny Thomas. David had made arrangements for us to stay with them until our married student housing was available. We had arrived three days too early to move into our new apartment. Larry, Jenny's husband, took Chris home while David scrambled through suitcases to find proper work clothes for the day. Before Chris left, he and Larry unhooked the U-Haul from the car so when David got ready to leave he wouldn't have to unhook it. I met and talked to Jenny while David got ready. She was very friendly and they had a three-year-old daughter named Karissa who was precious and very busy. She was already up when we arrived. David had finally regrouped. He told us he would be back for sure at noon, that he knew they wouldn't expect him to stay the whole day since he just got married. I kissed him at the door and he was off to his first day of work. I told Jenny I would love to talk more but I would just fall asleep if I stayed up any longer. I took a shower and crawled up into bed in their guest bedroom that would be our home for two days more.

I slept all day and David woke me up at 3:30 P.M. that afternoon. He was laughing, telling me how he fell asleep and nodded throughout the day. He got in bed with me and fell fast asleep. We slept through the evening and night into the next morning (Tuesday) before we woke up for him to go to work again the next day. I ate a little breakfast and crawled back into bed. I slept most of the day. When he came home I was playing with Karissa. He was so tired and sleepy, and we both went to bed early again. We woke early the next morning and I was too excited because we were moving into our married student apartment after work. After he left for work I got dressed and Jenny drove me to pick up the keys.

I had applied to the University of Northern Iowa to work on my master's degree. David insisted on me returning to school. I told him I was tired of school and he said, "No, you can't do anything else but get your degree right now." So when I stepped on that campus I was a not-so-happy camper. The campus was large, and I was unsure about matriculating here. Up to this time I had always attended African-American school environments. The enrollment was eleven thousand, and it was overwhelming. I said to myself, "You've got to do this because David wants you to, and Mom and Dad would be so proud too, and just think you won't be in class with eleven thousand at one time and be the one black speck in the crowd." I talked to myself a lot that day.

Jenny waited in the car while I got the key. When I returned we headed for our new address. We lived at 102 F Street. The apartment was clean with a living room/dining combination, kitchen, two bedrooms, and one bath. It was perfect, and I felt at home. David arrived and we began to unload the U-Haul. We stopped long enough to go purchase a mattress and box spring. Papa Jack had given us seven hundred dollars for our wedding gift, and we bought our first set of mattresses at Sears and Roebuck. We purchased a frame to place the mattress on and we had a bed for sure. I searched through the wedding gifts and found a set of sheets, being careful to keep the gift card so I could send thank-you notes later. The bed was soon ready and I also managed to find towels too and hung them in the bathroom. We ate out that night as we were too tired to do anything else.

When we lay in our own bed that night we laughed, talked, hugged, and kissed, and after four days of marriage we consummated the marriage bed. We fell fast asleep as naked as we came into the world. We loved each other so very much. My gynecologist had placed an IUD in my uterus for birth control, and the lovemaking was icing on the cake. Talking about cake: our cake top made it to Iowa and we put it in the freezer to save for our first wedding anniversary.

Years Before the Children

Our first few days of marriage were going great and they were busy with school and the like. David was teaching music at a junior high school, and that kept him very busy. He was also a minister of music at Janesville United Methodist Church in Janesville, Iowa. He had worked as their minister of music the year he was in graduate school, and he always integrated the church each Sunday. When our first Sunday came around for us to attend church together as a couple he told me what to expect. He also asked me to join the choir because he could use some more altos. When we arrived at the church it was a large brick church with a steeple and a cross. People were arriving in large numbers, and it looked like something I had seen at the movies. I was afraid for a moment but I thought to myself, "David has faced these people a whole year all by himself so how bad could it be?" Inside the church I was greeted with lots of smiles and people telling me how glad they were that David got married. The minister introduced me to the whole congregation and I was welcomed by all. At the end of church service I quickly moved toward David. One of his senior choir members said, "David, you sure did get you a pretty bed warmer," and we laughed. I had no idea what the winter would be like in Cedar Falls, Iowa.

Each day after classes I would rush home and prepare dinner. David would give me twenty-five dollars a week for groceries. I always manage to spend eighteen dollars and save the rest for something special. I didn't have to worry about having money for the beauty shop because there was no such thing as a black hair salon in Cedar Falls, Iowa. David would fix my hair for me sometimes because he had grown up in a beauty salon and had seen it done over and over again. Our supper time was special. I always served a salad, meat, vegetable greens, light or dark bread, cornbread or rolls. The meals would be enough for four people. We didn't like leftovers so we would eat everything I cooked every day. After dinner we would wash the dishes. I would study while David read the newspaper and listened to music. The weekends were special because we would go dancing and out to eat on Friday night and we would sleep most of the day on Saturday. We would go to bed naked and wake up to roll in the sheets and only move to go to the bathroom. David loved my breasts and I loved him to touch me all over. We spent a lot of time together. We were rarely ever apart. We shopped together, visited friends together; we were just together and truly in love. David's mother would call us almost every day. She really missed him because they were used to talking almost every day. When she would call, she would always tell me that she was glad he got married but she just had to talk to David because he was all she had. I learned within our first few weeks of marriage that, for him, being an only child was very stressful.

I was really enjoying my classes at the University of Northern Iowa. After all, I really didn't want to or have an interest in continuing, but David encouraged me to keep going. In each class I was always in the minority. Nobody would speak to me, and I could rarely ever get a smile. I had to make all my classes because if I missed a day, who would give me notes from the class I missed? It was a lonely place to be in. I would often say if I was not married and knew I had a black husband to go home to when I left this cold environment, it would be very difficult to keep showing up. After such cold treatment I decided that nothing would stop me from getting my degree. I was going to get it just because the other students weren't friendly.

One day after leaving class I met a girl named Sharon. We discovered we were married on the same day and time. We also lived one building from each other in married-student housing. She and her husband were from the same hometown. After about two months she began to say things like he is spending too much time with his friends or she would leave and go home without him on the weekends. Then she would say that they argued a lot. Soon I saw her very little. I thought to myself, "I am a fifteen-hour drive from home so I have to get along with my husband." She appeared to be a whining person and one who had not been taught to be strong. Just listening to her, I felt they couldn't hold on for one year.

Friday evening was Friday again, but this Friday was different. We had gone out dancing and to dinner and had returned home when Lonnie called. He asked David to meet him at the popular pizza place. It was already late so I told him to wake me up when he returned. He told me it was one of his white friends from graduate school. He didn't wake me when he returned; I just heard the shower running and drifted back to sleep. When morning came I asked him if they had a nice visit and he quietly said yes.

Saturdays were spent sleeping and later picking up groceries or going to the mall. During the week it was work as usual. One day after school, David came home to say that he knew he had lost his job. When I asked him why, he told me one of his seventh-grade students was singing but was doing more playing than singing so David grabbed him by his collar and shook him. He was so afraid that the parents would call the principal. I assured him that his action was noted by the students and I was sure a seventh grader in the wrong would not turn himself in to his parents.

The fall choir concert for the junior high students was coming. David pushed extra to get them ready. The big night came so I dressed in my Sunday best on that Thursday night. I went along with David and sat along the wall as the students arrived. They all had so much energy, and I could pick the problem student out of the crowd. I watched them come in until they were all in place. They had a real nice sound for such a young choir. You could tell by their sound that David had worked them hard. When they got ready to take a break before the real performance one of the students asked," I thought your wife was coming tonight." He told the students, "My wife is here," and they said, "Where?" He pointed to me and they said, "She looks like your daughter." I told them I would always be their friend. After talking to a lot of the kids, the concert was a big success. David still had a job, and the principal never called him in for jerking up the kid by his collar.

Winter was coming and I didn't know what to expect. I would see electrical plugs hanging out of the front of cars, snow tires, chains on tires, and people wearing extra clothing. In the South, if you saw white people wearing heavy coats you knew it would be below-zero temperatures because they never liked to wear coats. As blacks the first wind blows and we pull out bears and fur coats. Our ancestors taught us to keep warm when it is cold. I remember my grandmother saying, "If you dress half-naked now it will catch up with you in old age." When your grandmother or your mother said this, you had to wear a coat when you left the house even if you took it off out of their sight.

Thanksgiving was coming, and I was too excited with mid-terms behind me and a trip planned to Aunt Helen and Uncle Oliver's house in Milwaukee, Wisconsin. We had planned to visit them because they were the closest relatives to us in terms of driving distance. David was off the Wednesday before Thanksgiving so we planned to leave on Wednesday. Tuesday went so slowly all day long. I could hardly sleep that night because I was too excited. I would always be excited the night before I would have to go on a long trip. Morning finally came and I got up and opened the blinds like every morning. Only this morning it was twelve inches of snow on the ground! I began to cry and told David we couldn't go because it was snowing. You see, when it would snow an inch in Arkansas the whole city of Pine Bluff would close—schools, stores, and everything—so I was sure the roads were closed. David reminded me that it was the Midwest and that they had equipment to keep the roads open no matter how bad the snow got; they were prepared. I began to feel better and, for the first time in life, ready to take on the snow and not stay away from it. We loaded the car and secured the house for the long weekend. I talked to my mom and she told me to put a blanket in the trunk just in case of car trouble. When we hit the road David was right: the highway was all clear and we drove to keep up with the traffic. Stopping only for gas, we ventured on as the snow covered the shoulders of the highway. We reached a portion of the highway that was covered with snow and ice. David told me not to hit my brakes. The traffic was moving along very slowly when suddenly it came to a stop. I hit the brakes hard and we went off onto the shoulder on the opposite side of the road. I felt so stupid while David said, "I told you not to hit the brake," and I said, "It was either hit the brake or the car in front of me." As we were fussing, a highway snow blower came by and radioed ahead for a tow truck to come and pull us out. In the meanwhile a man came by in his personal truck and pulled us out. We wondered if we would have enough money to pay for him towing us out. I asked the gentleman what we owed him and he simply said to do something kind for someone else one day. We couldn't believe it. He had pulled us out so fast. He said on snowy days he would drive the highways and help people out. We knew God was looking out for us that day. We were back on the highway in minutes. On the road again, David drove the rest of the way. So much for my driving in the snow adventure.

We arrived in Milwaukee before dark. I was glad because my aunt and uncle worried about you when you came in at night. We parked the car in front of the house. It was just like coming home. I had spent many, many holidays with my aunt and uncle and all of my summers. They had no children so they asked my mother when I was born if I could be their child since I had an older brother and sister already. My parents agreed I could go with them as long as my school schedule was not interrupted. I always felt protected and like an only child when

I was with them. They had so much love for one another, and they displayed it all the time. It was always quiet conversation in their home and lots of hugs and kisses going on all the time. As we drove up all of the aforementioned came into my mind. I couldn't wait to see them.

We rang the door bell, and they both opened the door. We could hardly get in for all the excitement. This was the first time we had seen any family since we married in August. It was an awesome moment. The house smelled of fresh-baked bread and cakes. I knew she had been cooking, getting ready for the Thanksgiving meal. She told us that their good friends, the Hughes', would be over for dinner tomorrow. I didn't care who came; I just knew I couldn't wait to eat some real cooking. We talked all evening. David and Uncle Oliver went to the store while Aunt Helen and I talked about everything. I told her I loved being married, and she said that even though she waited so long she loved it too. We smiled and hugged some more. Aunt Helen prepared a light dinner so we all ate and talked some more before retiring for the night. I could tell we were tired because we kissed each other and fell asleep.

Thanksgiving morning came, and I got up early to talk to Uncle Oliver while Aunt Helen and David slept late. Uncle and I were always early risers while Aunt Helen would sleep till 10:00 A.M. She would plainly tell you not to wake her up before 10:00 A.M. We talked about Iowa and school and I told him how I was afraid we wouldn't get to come to visit because of the snow. He laughed and said, "You people from down south never move when it snows. Here we just pull out the snow plows and move the snow out of the way." We continued to talk about past memories, and we sang a song or two from my childhood days and laughed so hard. No matter what time of year it was, we always sang, "I ain't getting nothing for Christmas 'cause I ain't been nothing but bad" and he would sing "North to Alaska." Those are warm, fuzzy memories. Soon we began preparing breakfast, and those who were sleeping could sleep no more.

Aunt Helen and David came in for breakfast. Uncle and I told them how much fun we had been having. They both smiled. When breakfast was finished Uncle Oliver gave Aunt Helen a very big kiss on the jaw. He would do this after every meal. It was the most precious thing to see. Such love to have is all one could think of when you saw such an act of love portrayed in this way. It was our first Thanksgiving to be married, and we helped to prepare the meal. David and Uncle were going to the store or watching the football games. I set the table. Just setting the table at Aunt Helen's house was almost always stressful because you had to set each place setting according to the etiquette books. She was a home economics major, and she had been well-trained and knew how that table should look. After I finished, I asked her to check that table, and I passed with flying colors. I was amazed because sometimes she would fix just a few things, by straightening them up. We began to put the turkey, dressing, home-grown green beans, candied sweet potatoes, greens, cranberry salad, cornbread, scratch rolls, macaroni and cheese, cranberry sauce, pound cake, peach cobbler, and iced tea to drink on the table. We sat down and Uncle Oliver blessed the food. He would always say, "O merciful Father we thank you for this food that it may nourish us and strengthen. Bless all the sick and shut in and bless this food for the nourishment of our bodies for Christ sake. Amen." Then he would quote a Bible verse until all seated had recited one. I always hoped we wouldn't pray too long for fear the food would get cold. When the praying ended I could hardly wait for the food to be passed. Just to taste some home cooking was a special treat since I was so far from my mom's cooking. Aunt Helen was a great cook. My plate was so full and when I finished eating I could hardly move. Uncle Oliver teased me about eating one food at a time. I would eat one food at a time and turn my plate until I had finished eating each food. I had done this for as long as I could remember. When we had eaten all we could hold, we sat and talked about school, Iowa, and our plans for Christmas. Aunt

Helen and Uncle Oliver said they were so very proud of us. The phone rang, and it was David's mom and dad to wish us a happy Thanksgiving. Everyone was doing fine in Memphis. Later that night my mom and dad called and everyone was doing fine. Dad bragged about how good his dressing was so we teased and laughed about that. I told Mom about us slipping off the road and she asked, "Did you have a blanket in the car like I told you?" and I said, "Yes." And I smiled. After dinner dishes were cleared from the table we seemed to wash dishes for two hours and we had so much food to put away. Aunt Helen had already told me she was sending food home with us.

That Friday after Thanksgiving I slept late, and we just talked that day and began to listen to the weather reports. The weatherman was reporting a severe snowstorm for Saturday night and Sunday. We had planned to go to church with them on Sunday but we left on Saturday morning because of the impending snowstorm. Aunt Helen had packed most of the Thanksgiving left-overs in our car. We left around noon and drove straight through, only stopping for gas. I dialed Aunt Helen and Uncle Oliver to let them know we had arrived safely. They were happy. We thanked them for a wonderful Thanksgiving. We were glad to be home alone again because we would never get to be intimate away from home. We rolled in the sheets Saturday night and made up for those lost moments of sharing our body. When we awoke on Sunday morning, we had blizzard-like conditions. You couldn't see anything. The wind howled and blew and blew. I was so glad we had food because I was not leaving the house that Sunday. By Monday morning the schools were closed because of the snow. I told David that was great because I could sleep in late. He told me, "Your classes at the university never close because of a storm so you better get dressed and get going." I put on long underwear and layered my clothing, sweater, coat, and boots. I got out into the snow, and it was blowing so hard I could hardly stand. I walked two miles to school in that blizzard. When I reached my building, I said, "This university is granting me a degree just for going to class in a blizzard." When I entered the building and went to my class several other crazy people like me had braved the storm and made it to class. I knew that November day after having to be coerced into graduate school and dealing with the subtle racism, I was going to get my master's degree. That storm made me angry enough to seriously take my schooling all the way.

When I arrived back home David said, "Well, you've made it through your first snowstorm." He teased me and I told him, "I just can't see how I made it."

The weeks between Thanksgiving and Christmas flew by because David was busy preparing Christmas concert music and I was getting ready for final exams. On Wednesday nights we would travel to Janesville, Iowa, for choir rehearsal. David was using several pieces from Handel's *Messiah*. We had sung the entire *Messiah* throughout our choir days in college. At rehearsal, David and I would always eye one another and sometimes we would laugh and only the two of us knew why we were laughing. One time in rehearsal, Mr. George was singing the baritone solo and David looked at me and I began to laugh. David laughed and we couldn't stop. When he finally stopped I was still laughing. He began to look at me and I could tell he was serious. I soon regained my composure. Rehearsal was soon over and because I had laughed so much, David wouldn't talk to me, he only said, "Let's go home." In the car it was quiet. I tried to humor him at times but I could tell he was embarrassed by our uncontrolled laughter. When he did speak, all he said was we shouldn't have laughed. I told him it's just hard to listen to Mr. George sing without laughing. The next week came and I bit my tongue so I wouldn't laugh when he sang his baritone solo.

The Sunday before Christmas came and we sang beautifully in the morning worship. We were glad to get it over with because school was out for David and I had completed my finals. We were going home finally to see our family since we left from our wedding day. We packed and loaded the car and, believe me, I had a blanket in the car. We drove from Cedar Falls to St. Louis, Missouri, and got a nice hotel room and spent the night. In our hotel room was a king-sized bed. I remember not being able to sleep well because we were not close to one another. David called his cousin Ginger and from what I had been told, everyone was afraid of her and her children. They seemed to be the bad people in the family. They didn't bother to come and see us at the hotel. I was glad because I had heard all kinds of horror stories about this family.

Morning came and after grabbing a quick breakfast in bed we checked out and headed straight to Memphis. The weather was great and it felt so good to be south again where even the brown grass and trees looked better than the white snow. We spent a week in Memphis and a week in Pine Bluff. We visited every relative and friend in Memphis and attended church with Miss Susie, as I fondly called her. All her nieces and nephews, because they were so close to her in age, called her Susie. Miss Susie was a beautician and was in her beauty shop a lot. The beauty shop was just next door. She offered to fix my hair, so while she was doing so, we talked about what was happening in Memphis and I talked about school, David, and myself. Miss Susie told me that she was sorry to call us so much but she just needed to talk to him often. She said they had been through a lot and she just wanted to keep in touch. She said to me, "I'm glad you're his wife," I guess trying to convince herself that I was truly a part of the family. She finished my hair in between four other people so I went to the house to see David. Papa Jack, who was David's grandfather (his father's father), would always lecture us about being good and loving toward one another. He wanted us to stay together and work hard. David's father had a lot of respect for me. He would always watch me carefully and watched how I carried myself. On occasion he would call me Miss Deborah. We spent most of our evening visiting relatives and David's class-mates and seeing some of our college classmates.

Monday came and we headed for Pine Bluff. I had already told my parents we were on the way. They could hardly wait to see us. My brother Matthew met us at the door. He was a teenager and was giving Mom and Dad a hard way to go; plus being the only child at home added to that. When I saw my mom I hugged her and hugged her. It was as if we had been apart for years. Dad was in the grocery store, and we went out to see him. He was overjoyed too that we had made it home. He teased us both about adding some pounds on since we first got married. David stayed in the store with Daddy while I went to talk to Mom. I couldn't wait to see my nieces. I asked Mom if they were coming over and she said yes but she wasn't sure when. I called my brother James and my sister-in-law Denise and let them know we had arrived safely. I told them to let me talk to the girls, and they were asking me to come and get them. They couldn't believe I was back. I am sure for them it was like a loss when I left after I married and not seeing me for months. I missed them tremendously.

After lunch David and I went to see James, Denise, and the girls. After a brief visit we took the girls with us back to Mom's. We played and we ate ice cream and popcorn until bedtime. We were simply glad to see one another. We went through our nightly routine of playing in the bathtub and comb-ing, brushing, and braiding hair before bedtime. Then it was time to tuck everybody in. These were the sweetest little girls I knew, and they would fall fast asleep after a little drink of water and a quick bathroom break. After tucking those little ones in I went down stairs to talk to Mom and Dad, David, and Matthew. We sat and watched TV, ate popcorn, and talked about everything. We shared our stories about the snow while my brother Matthew talked about his new girlfriend. Mom and I got up and went to her bedroom and left the guys to talk. She showed me all the new clothes she had made for me and for my nieces. Mom's sewing is second to none. My mom, I've always thought, can make anything. She is just that talented. We looked at new dress patterns and thumbed through some old ones, too. Mom could make my clothes fit my body and David could buy my clothes and the ones he purchased fit like a glove. Boy, they just knew my body. David had excellent taste in clothes, and he knew just what would look right on me. After talking about the dresses, patterns, and materials, I tried on a few of the new things she had sewn for me. Just as always, they fit perfectly. Time came and I went upstairs and got in bed. David came on later. That next morning we awoke to three little smiling faces patting on our cover wanting to get in bed with us. They climbed in and went back to sleep for a short period. When it was finally time to get up I always dressed the girls, washed their face, brushed their teeth, and combed their hair before I would ever get dressed. They often would ask, "When are you going to put your clothes on?" and I would reply, "After I get you all dressed up." My precious nieces taught me how to serve and how to love and protect. When everyone was finished and dressed I would always send them downstairs and Mom always had breakfast waiting for them. By the time I would finish dressing and get downstairs they would already be playing.

Our time in Pine Bluff seemed so brief and with our daily routine of visiting each evening, between preparing meals and shopping and seeing relatives, it was time to head back to Memphis. We spent a night in Memphis and then headed for Cedar Falls. We drove straight through. I drove the bulk of the miles because David would get so sleepy on the highway, no matter how much sleep he'd had the night before.

Back in Cedar Falls, it was cold and snowy, and the regular routine of school and work began again. After settling in, the phone rang and it was Lonnie asking David to meet him at the pizza parlor again. I told him I would wait up on him and he had no response, only "I will see you later." I remember this happening a few more evenings so I felt the need to talk to him. I told David to tell Lonnie that he had a wife and that his evenings were for her. Lonnie never called again after I said that.

School was going great until, one day, David quit his teaching job. He said he could not teach music to people who could not appreciate it. He wrote up a proposal for the Waterloo Recreation and Arts Commission and presented it to them. They hired David on the spot as the music arts coordinator for the art center. I, too, got lucky and landed a job working as a Women's, Infant, and Children's nutritionist for Operation Threshold. During the second semester of graduate school, all my classes were at night from 7:00 to 10:00 P.M. I worked daily from 8:00 A.M. to 4:30 P.M. We were both very industrious and working in our chosen fields. Life was going well.

January 19, 1978, just happened to be my twenty-first birthday. That morning we got up and David and I were busy cleaning the apartment. While cleaning I discovered a case of champagne under the second bedroom bed. I knew David was planning a surprise party for me but I just didn't know when. After cleaning all morning I took a brief nap and we went on our usual Saturday shopping. When we returned and put everything away David told me he wanted to take me to dinner. We went to the Boar's Head, which was a very expensive restaurant. They served wonderful steaks and we ate filet mignon for my birthday dinner. After dinner we drove slowly home and I teased him in the car on the way home about how I would repay him in bed for such a special treat. We drove up and parked in our usual parking space. David unlocked and opened the door and people were inside screaming "Surprise." I acted surprised but I wasn't really since I had discovered the champagne that morning. Most of our Iowa friends were there, and the cake was beautiful. I remember feeling so special. When the last person left I kissed and hugged him so that, by the time we got to the bedroom, we were both in our birthday suits. I felt so special. I thanked him for a wonderful evening and he said I deserved it. The next day at church, choir members had birthday cards for me, and the Herbert family invited us over for Sunday dinner. The Herberts had children around or about our ages and they were so good to us. We felt so welcomed even when we knew we were the minorities. They never made a big deal over us being a minority. After dinner at the Herberts we drove back to Cedar Falls. We mostly rested and I studied. I just remember it being the best birthday ever. David always gave me a card and wrote me a letter. He was such a poet, and I always enjoyed his cards and letters. He always knew just what to say.

My work with the WIC program was going great. I used my clients to do my master's research project while on the job. I researched the "Effects of the Women's, Infants, and Children's Supplemental Food Program on Cedar Falls Participants." The study returned very positive results as my advisor approved the idea. As the end of the spring semester approached, I resigned my job as WIC nutritionist to complete my graduate studies. I had six hours remaining to complete the program requirements. The people I worked with at the WIC office were sad to see me leave, but I was on a mission and completing the master's degree was in my plan. The summer was medium-cool to hot some days, and the Iowa corn fields' crickets would sing you to sleep. I remember one night one cricket was inside the apartment. We would get up and turn the light on and the cricket would get quiet. When we would turn the light off it would began to sing again. It took fifteen minutes or longer to find that cricket. Once we found him we would hit him and jump when the cricket would jump toward us. We were laughing so hard because we were both hitting and jumping. When we finally silenced him we were still laughing about what we went through to get him quiet.

Because I had finished college at the University of Arkansas at Pine Bluff in the summer I was supposed to return to Pine Bluff to march in the spring commencement. After discussing the length of the trip we decided, instead, to go to Minneapolis, Minnesota. We had a wonderful weekend even though it rained cats and dogs all the way. The Mid-America Mall was the largest indoor mall I had ever seen. We called and spoke briefly with Deana. She was the aunt to my bridesmaid Lenora. It was good to speak to her. Minneapolis was fun, and I felt David was trying to make up for not taking me to my college graduation. I was fine and I understood what it would take to get us there.

I completed all my requirements and passed my written exams. The University of Northern Iowa didn't offer summer commencement so I would have to return in May 1979 to participate in the graduation exercise.

We contemplated our next move. David said that he wanted to move to Nashville to study for a Ph.D. in music education at George Peabody College for Teachers. We had finished and met our goals in Iowa. When we began to pack for our move to Tennessee, we realized we had accumulated a lot of things. We loaded the car and it was full. It was too full to pull the U-Haul. I went back into the house and David had given my stuffed animals I had since high school to some little kids going down the street. I went up to them and said, "He really didn't mean to give you my stuffed toys; he's just frustrated because we have so much to move." Our friends Janice and Johnny McCullough let us use their van while they kept our car and we had our problem solved. We did leave behind a couch, mattress, and box spring.

We always enjoyed our road trips. I loved Lay's potato chips and David would buy me a Coke and a bag of Lay's each time we stopped for gas. We had planned ahead for married-student housing. When we arrived in Nashville our housing would not be available for six weeks. Nashville was such an impressive city to me after living in flat Iowa for a year. It was a welcomed change. We only knew one couple in Nashville, and that was Derrick and Candice Trout. Candice was the sister to Joyce Brown who was married to my home boy, Rodney Hinkley. Joyce was my special sister because she trained me through my teenage years. Candice and Derrick were very kind to us. They helped us find an apartment, and they had a seven-year-old son affectionately called Ronnie. Ronnie was such a mature little fellow, and he knew his way all over Nashville. A lot of the time Candice would ask him where to turn and he would be right. We found an apartment in Laurel Hills in Hermitage, Tennessee. It was thirteen miles from Nashville, but it was all we could find before David was scheduled to begin the program. The Trouts were so warm, friendly, sharing, and caring. They opened their home to us just as if we had known them all our lives. There was no pretending. We felt at home.

After spending a few nights with the Trouts we moved to the Laurel Hills apartment's ground floor. I hated it because it was dark and damp. I told myself: only a few weeks.

David went to George Peabody College and met with his advisor. He had a full load of classes and had entered as a full-time student. I was busy trying to find employment. I took a job working near home at the McKendree Manor Nursing Home. I was hired as a salad maker. When I was interviewed they told me I was over-qualified, and I told them I knew that but I needed a job and I knew how to work hard. Henry Williams, my dad, taught me how to work hard in the grocery store. I worked daily from 6:30 A.M. to 3:00 P.M. The job was going well when one day the manager called me in and told me there was a job at Parkview Hospital as a food service supervisor. I told her I would go for the interview. They hired me on the spot and I was just across from Vanderbilt's campus, which contained the George Peabody College campus. I knew once our married-student housing was ready it would be close enough to walk if I needed to.

We kept a busy schedule, and the apartment seemed so far away from school and work. When we would leave in the morning we would plan to be gone all day. We learned to eat, sleep, and dress in the car. After nearly six weeks of living in Hermitage, Tennessee, we got our first visit from David's mom and cousins. Being a new bride I wanted to make sure my home was clean and organized. I wanted to impress my mother-in-law and my new cousins-in-law as much as I possibly could. We didn't have much, but what we had, we put together. When they arrived, everything was in place so we chatted and David was glad to see everyone and so was I. I prepared dinner that night of spaghetti, green beans, salad, and rolls. We laughed and ate and talked for a while. I went to bed after cleaning the kitchen, leaving David and his mother up to talk. We were up early to go sight-seeing in Nashville. With the city being pretty new to us we were ready to make new discoveries. We all got up and dressed. I remember cooking bacon, eggs, and toast, and they really didn't eat much. David's family was pretty picky when it comes to eating. After breakfast we headed for downtown Nashville. We saw the Country Music Hall of Fame, Fort Nashborough, Printers Alley, the State Capitol, and Legislative Plaza. The town felt good, and I felt we would do well here.

After being out the whole day we headed back to Hermitage. As we began to talk about dinner, my mother-in-law said she would cook. Her famous menu was fried chicken, greens, sweet potatoes, and hot-water cornbread. As she cooked I was keeping the kitchen clean. After dinner, I began to feel frustrated because my few newlywed pots and pans were all burned up or food was stuck on them from boiling over the sides. You see, my mom always took care of the pots and pans, and we spent a lot of time scrubbing them to make sure they were clean inside and outside. A burned pot never sat on our stove. Just looking at the mess I had to clean up was bringing back those old memories of pot scrubbing. While they sat and talked, I scrubbed pot after pot. By the time I finished I went to bed and cried because my pots had been fully broken in. I decided that I never wanted my mother-in-law to cook in my house again because it put too much work on me. After rolling out of bed and preparing breakfast once again they began to pack up and traveled back to Memphis. David had spent a lot of time with his family while I stayed busy in the kitchen. After their entire first visit to us weren't all pots.

By October 1978 our married-student housing was finally ready. We were so glad to move from Hermitage to stop making the long drive into Nashville each day. We moved to 1109A 18th Avenue South. We were in a duplex, and it was an older home. The duplex had a living room with fireplace, dining room, kitchen, two bedrooms upstairs, a small study room, and a bathroom. Once we moved everything in, we were right at home. It was roomy with high ceilings. I was so glad to be in walking distance of most things. David would walk to class most days after dropping me off at work at Parkview Hospital.

The Parkview Hospital working experience opened my eyes to a whole new world. I had completed my master's so when I came to work at Parkview, the dietitians there were intimidated by me because not one of them had a master's degree. Mrs. Beverly Day was director of dietetics. She was an okay white lady but she had her ways, too. After being there for a month I asked to meet with her. I told Mrs. Day I wanted to pursue my dietetic registration and explained to her how working experience under two registered dietitians would count toward my being able to meet the requirements. This method of getting licensed was called a dietetic traineeship program. Mrs. Day agreed that she and Sally Evans would help me with the program. They both filled out the necessary paperwork and the process had begun. I never expected the challenges I faced but I had to face them.

I came to learn that working in dietetics you meet some people who come from various backgrounds and experiences like none I had ever seen before. I was treated with certain coldness in the kitchen because the blacks in the kitchen were jealous of me because I had knowledge and I could speak in the office among whites and work with those who would let me. There were women there who supported me totally and always told me they were so proud because they never had anyone in the kitchen, black, who had the education I had. There was Mattie Kline who had eight children. There was Miss Jerry

Harris and Miss Lucy and Dear Miss Yvonne who had four
of the most beautiful girls. All these women encouraged me
in the midst of a lot of racist actions toward me by blacks and
whites. Because I worked in the kitchen, the blacks who were
there didn't want to train me. They would always say if I asked
a question, "You should know that already," or if I made a mis-
take they made sure it got to the office as to set me up for trouble. There was Mary Holt, Emily Tate, and Tommie who always
hung together and who worked hard to make it hard for me.
They would stand on the patient tray line and push trays past me
before I could put an item on the tray or check it and then laugh
and say, "You missed that." The white office staff was always
nice but you knew it was just surface. Jamie, Andrea, and Miss
Bennett worked on the hospital floors visiting patients, and if I
was allowed to go on the floor I had to make a visit with them.
Andrea was a good white woman who always told me the inside
politics. Miss Bennett, on the other hand, would tell me that I
would work and help my husband get through school and then
he would leave me. Knowing that I had to take the registration
exam at the end of the traineeship, she would always point out
the pass/failure rate to me in the *American Dietetic Association
Journal.* She was a very insecure woman and worked hard to
create situations like hers with others. Jamie was neither hot
nor cold. Loving her husband and daughter was mostly her conversation for the day. Alex, the only white man who was over
Production and Ordering, was neat. He saw in me what others
refused to see: a person. He would always call me by name and
was always telling me to tell my husband to take me to different restaurants. A lot of his suggestions proved to be true. He
would always smile and was just a neat person to work with
who seemed to be blind to what I was experiencing on the job.

I worked every shift so I could learn all the areas. The
evening part-time employees were mostly teenagers and adults
who were coming to their second jobs. There was Beth, a
middle-aged woman, who would always wear a tight uniform

and roll her hips for the young teenage boys. Beth would sing, dance, play, and finally work. She told us one evening while working on the tray line that she only dated married men and that her married men have to see her late at night. She said at first he was on top and then she said, "I told him let me ride for a while." I thought I would crawl under the table. She went on to say that while she was riding his eyes went into the back of his head so she got off because she thought he was having a heart attack and she didn't want to be the woman who killed him, although she knew her loving was good. After explaining all this, she said she got up and got dressed and got out of his house before his wife came home. She was so proud of her story that she began to twist and shake across the floor. By this time everyone was laughing or just plainly had lost it. I had never in my life heard of such a mess in all my life. But this was life in dietetics. Miss Coral and Miss Lucy were super cooks. The food was always good. I had my first taste of fried eggplant, and Miss Coral taught me how to make it. I made it at home, and David liked it too.

Miss Mattie, with the eight children, always encouraged me. She would say she wished she had gone to school and had a different life from her many children. She was unique in that she worked hard and the children she had who were of working age were working and working hard. She worked two jobs daily. Every day she would wake up her children and tell them get up and you better not miss the bus. Sometimes they would call back and would have gotten into a fight with another sibling. She would fuss and tell them, "You wait till I see you this evening after I get off from work." She could threaten them almost to death just with her tone of voice. Miss Mattie was a mother who truly was trying all by herself. There were days I would cry about how I was being treated and she would drag me into the bathroom and tell me, "Don't let them see you cry. I know it's hard but don't let them see you cry and remember them old kitchen Negroes will be here when you are long gone on to your way to the top." Seeing her helped me, and seeing me seemed to help her. She really pushed her kids to go to school and stay in school. Miss Mattie was a supervisor but she loved to fry chicken. Before she would fry that chicken she would wash it over and over again until it almost looked like something else you couldn't put a name to, but that chicken would be cleaned and fried to perfection. She never said this to me and I never asked her, but I bet that frying chicken was what she learned to cook first. We had a special bond, and when it got tough in that Parkview kitchen I could find solace in her.

David would pick me up daily from work. We would both go home and study. Sometimes we would eat and some days there would not be much we wanted to eat. My job was only paying seven thousand dollars a year; he was full-time and was working five part-time music jobs and made almost as much as I did on one job and he was a full-time student. We came home sometimes just to re-dress and go to church for choir rehearsal. Then there were Friday nights when we hit the Radisson Hotel for disco dancing. Friday night was much fun. There were times when we went to parties with some of his George Peabody classmates and professors. I was always a quiet presence feeling inadequate to participate in their intellectual conversations. I perfected a smooth nod, and that kept me in. On occasion a wife or girlfriend would come up to have conversation, and it would feel more comfortable. When they realized David was an excellent singer, they would always ask him to sing "Sunshine" by John Denver. We would never overstay at a party when we were in the minority because we always feared once white folks pulled their beer out and forgot themselves they may remember who we were and call us a "nigger" so we always left before the beer was served.

Calling home each week, I would check on my parents and they would be excited to hear from us. My dad would encourage me to hang in there. He would say, "Baby, you got to crawl before you walk," and I would respond by saying, "But Daddy,

I am lying down," and that would tickle him. He would tell me, "They have what you want so get it from them and they can't take it away." There were days when David would pick me up from work that I would just get in the car and lie over on him and cry. The mental games in that kitchen some days would be too much to bear.

David was in school with people twice his age, and they all told stories about children, dogs, cats, and other animals. David came home one day and told me that we were either going to have a baby or we were going to get a dog. I thought, "I am not having a baby now in the middle of all this mess of school and work." Well, when he picked me up one day from work, there in the car with him was Deanna LaRu Walker, a black and white miniature collie, beautiful and quite friendly. She was our first addition to our little family unit. We fell out because he wanted the dog inside and I wanted the dog outside. I guess you know she stayed inside, but I would not allow her upstairs. Sweeping hair was an everyday chore, but she would meet you at the door just too happy to see you. She was a great pet.

On Friday night David told me he wanted us to go to the movie. When our money was long we could do things like that. We went to see *Making Love* with Roberta Flack's title song. The movie was about a couple who fell in love and married and who had a great friendship and wonderful love relationship. The movie seemed to be going great until it took a strange turn. The husband was bisexual, and his wife caught him in bed with another man. They divorced, but she loved him still so much she named her first baby by her second husband after him. I remember during the bisexual sex scenes closing my eyes and feeling really uncomfortable and trying to think why we came to see this movie. After the movie and riding home David asked me if I liked the movie and I said, "No." We never brought the movie up again.

I worked every other weekend and he worked every weekend with a choir or church group. We both loved church.

Our friends Derrick and Candice had taken us to church with them so we joined their church, First Baptist Capitol Hill. This church was a pillar of the community, having developed a lot of history during the civil rights movements. The style of worship was what I was accustomed to. We met so many people, and they seemed to understand a young married couple trying to go to school, and the struggle it involved. Reverend George Brown Hayes was pastor of the church, and he was an excellent preacher. His wife Sonya Hayes took us in as if we were her own because we were around the ages of their children. We would visit in their home quite often. They were people filled with lots of knowledge and much wisdom. Dr. Bernice Best, our choir director, was glad to have us in the church choir because we were certainly an asset. She loved us so much that one night at choir rehearsal she allowed me to tell the choir members what I was going through at work, and they prayed for me. It meant so much to me. Georgia Benson, the church organist, only kept encouraging words and she would always say, "I know you and David are going to make it." Going there at the time, it was all I could do to smile and say that I believed it.

Work, school, work, school, and Friday night was all we had time for. We always tried to go dancing or eat out on Fridays. When our money was short we would go and hang out with other poor graduate students like ourselves. Linda Barrett, a friend from childhood who is actually my sister's age, would always come over. She always wanted me to fix her a grilled cheese sandwich. She loved my grilled cheese sandwiches so much. I liked Linda because she was quiet and laid back and we always had fun. She and David had a few classes together. They would always talk about the classes, the professors, and just being black at Vanderbilt.

After almost eighteen months I began to study for the April 1980 Dietitian's Registration Exam. I studied everything that had the word *nutrition* on it. I had no study partner so I was on my own. The two dietitians who were working with me on the job had no encouragement for me. Mrs. Bennett showed me the pass/failure rate the day before the exam. I asked, "God, please help me pass the exam just to show them that not helping me didn't or couldn't stop me."

The day of the exam came. I was all too ready to go and get the exam over with. I was stressed but ready to put down all I had crammed into my head. The exam was held at the Law Lecture Hall on the Vanderbilt University campus. Upon my arrival I signed in and made sure I had my #2 pencils. There were people mingling in the hallway and talking to each other. People were asking each other how many times they had taken the exam. I overheard one lady say this was her fourth time to sit for the exam while another said, "It's my third." I whispered a prayer and said, "God, I don't have sixty-five dollars to throw away on taking an exam over. Lord, help me please!" The test monitor announced for us to take our seats. She explained the instructions for the exam and told us we could open our test booklets. The test consisted of five parts: clinical nutrition, community nutrition, child nutrition, food production, and equipment. The test consisted of one hundred seventy-five questions, and your passing score had to be one hundred fifty and above. Well after three hours I had answered as many questions as I could. I looked over my test briefly and turned it in. I felt so relieved and just glad the test and stress was over. I remember saying, "I don't care what I made on that test; I'm just glad it's over." That evening David took me to Spats for dinner. We had a lot of fun, and David could tell I was more relaxed. He said, "I will be glad when my dissertation is completed," and I replied, "It won't be long." Although I was relieved, I still had two long weeks ahead to wait on the test results. Each day I would go home and look for the mail. My work schedule had been changed to 11:30 A.M. to 8:00 P.M., so it was late when I got home daily. David would go home and check the mail. While working the late shift I was called to the main office. The secretary said, "I have your husband on the phone." I said,

"Hello" and David said, "I just thought you would want to know that you passed the Dietitians Registration Exam." I threw the phone down and I was screaming and crying. People came out of the kitchen to see what was wrong. I was screaming so much I couldn't talk when people were asking me what was wrong. I even heard someone say her mother must have died and I shook my head "no." They didn't know what to do with me. After about five minutes of screaming and crying I could only speak, "I passed, I passed, I passed!" I managed to call David back and all I could say was "I passed, I passed" and he was saying, "Yes, isn't it wonderful and I'm so proud of you." I told him thanks for letting me know but I teased him because I didn't do anything but scream when he told me and they just had to hang the phone up. He said it sounded like you were tearing up the place. After talking to him I went to find Miss Mattie to tell her. She began to jump and cry too because she had seen me go through so much. We just hugged and cried. The word spread that I had passed. Mrs. Bennett came and said, "I have a friend who has taken the exam four times and has not passed. She asked what she should do. I told her to tell her friend to just study everything that has *nutrition* written on it. That night when I got home I called my parents, and they too were excited. It was another proud parent moment. I was too excited to sleep. I couldn't believe it. I passed and I passed on the first try. God truly answered my prayer.

The next day when I went to work, I took my exam pass notice with me so the dietitians could see it. They said, "You not only passed, but you really scored well." All I could do was smile. After about a week of bliss I decided to call Mrs. Laura Heights, who was head dietitian at Meharry Medical College. Mrs. Heights told me she had a position open as administrative dietitian and would love to have me join her staff. I agreed. I thought to work at a historically black institution would be just what I needed to bring myself esteem and zeal back. I had been beaten down by hard racism by those who agreed to train me and not accepted by my own because they knew I was passing through. But you know when those black counterparts with whom I worked in the kitchen found out I had passed they were proud and became nicer overnight. It was so strange. I gave Parkview Hospital a two-week notice. I had planned my vacation time, and my letter arrived in Mrs. Day's office while I was away. No one knew why or where I was going, and they had to wait a whole week before anyone could find out. I had spoken with no one.

During my week of vacation David had a vocal music recital in Savannah, Georgia. We drove all night to get there. The Savannah State campus is truly awesome. We met with Dr. Brock, who was chairman of the music department. He was a white professor at a predominately black institution and just loved music and the students he worked with. He knew David from George Peabody, and he was proud to have David come as a role model for students studying music. Between rehearsals we had time to go to the beach and put our feet in the water and sand. It was so relaxing to be away from the normal routine. I kept thinking in my mind what was being said about me since no one knew why I was resigning. I would just smile to myself, saying I only have one more week in that pit. And it's going to be great when I get back. David's preparation for the concert had paid off, and he did an excellent job. He got a standing ovation and so much hand clapping until he had to do an encore number. His lyric tenor voice was so strong and getting stronger every day. We returned to Nashville, cleaning the house, grocery shopping and relaxing and listening to the recital tapes. David, of course, a perfectionist, was criticizing himself, and I kept saying, "Give yourself a break. The boy on that tape is bad and I'm going to go out with him and marry him some day," and he smiled.

Monday morning I couldn't wait to get dressed in my uniform and report to work. I had one week to work. When I came in Mrs. Day called me in her office and scolded me for going on vacation and mailing in a letter of resignation. She knew it was nothing more she could do. I had succeeded, and they looked for me to fail. I came out of her office thinking I had come in a lying-down state and would leave in a standing state. At this point, nothing she could say or do would hurt me. While I was away she had already hired someone to take my place and I told them to listen and learn fast because I only have a week to train you over what I've done for eighteen months. She only smiled. I was surprised with a department going-away party. Cake, punch, cookies, nuts, and roses were presented to me. I was just too happy. Later that night I learned Mattie had provided everything for the party and Mrs. Day threatened for fire her because she did it without departmental approval. Mattie and I hugged and laughed and she, staying behind, could only say, "Just keep going and don't look back and just keep in touch with me."

Reporting to my new job on Monday morning was quite exciting. I had my own office, and for the first time in my career the employees were addressing me as "Mrs. Walker." Every time I heard them say that my self-esteem and self-worth was climbing. You know it's just no place like home when you need a healing. Meharry Hubbard Hospital was more than just a job; it was an opportunity to help my own people, and while I was helping them, they, without knowing it, were providing much-needed healing for me. Mrs. Alaina Timothy was Mrs. Heights's secretary, and she was so proud of me. She often talked about her own children and how she was taking classes too. Fanny and Lock were the clinical dietitians. I covered the training of new employees, continuing education, and patient tray line. I looked forward to going to work every day. When I arrived these people had smiles on their faces and a story to tell daily. Someone was always reporting on a new love life, a new baby, and children, or reporting a ham was found in the dumpster. It was never a dull moment. To me, Meharry Hubbard was just the place to be. I called my Dad and told him about my new job and he said, "You can't gain much from moving from job to job," and I told him, "Daddy I just needed a change." Plus I told him, "Now, Dr. Hank Foster your former home boy, is a physician here and he can help look out for me. He said okay and seemed to be at ease after we had talked for a while. He just ended his conversation by saying, "You just watch after those Negroes because they can be something else." I laughed and we said goodbye.

David continued to work on his dissertation and study for his oral exams. Our summer was quickly passing by. It seemed as though people knew David was a rare individual of twenty-four years of age getting a doctorate in program and staff development administration and undergraduate and graduate degrees in music. People were calling him and offering him jobs from all over the country. I kept telling him, "We came to Nashville to get a Ph.D., and too many people leave at the dissertation level and never finish writing. We are poor now and we are used to it and we will just remain poor until we get that Ph.D." I would remind him of this and he would smile and say you're right.

The day finally came for David to take his oral exams. Dr. Rachel Wells from Bethune Cookman College had called us several times making offers. She even called during his oral exams to see if he had passed so she could offer him an assistant professorship of music.

I had taken off to be with David that day and we walked over to campus holding hands. When we arrived the committee greeted me and asked David to come in. I sat and waited and whispered prayers. David knew his stuff and he was super-intelligent and he knew so much information and had excellent recall level. I was confident he would come out shining. After about two hours the door opened and I could see them and hear them telling David congratulations. I knew he had passed. He immediately called Dr. Wells to let her know the results. She was quite pleased and she told him his application was in the mail. In all the excitement I never thought about leaving Nashville or my new job. When the excitement settled I began to grieve privately, never letting David know I really didn't want to leave Nashville. When I told Mrs. Heights that I was moving to Florida, it saddened her and the rest of the staff. In the short three months a bond had developed that we all felt encouraging me to move ahead. Meharry had the biggest going-away party for me. The president of the college wished me well as well as several other physicians. I had gifts, food, and you name it from everywhere. The people of Meharry truly showed their love for me. I really needed that after going through eighteen months of subtle abuse at Parkview Hospital. Membership at First Baptist Capitol Hill and being in the choir meant saying goodbye to them also. We told them we would miss them a lot. We had been a very active young couple in the church so the congregation gave us a going away love offering of seven hundred dollars. It truly came in handy on the move to Florida.

I wondered how we could move with our dog, DeAnna LaRue. As I began to sweep and mop the floors Dee kept running in and out so I put her out on the back porch of our duplex. I continued to sweep and mop. Once finished I went to bring Dee back in and she was gone from the porch. My heart went into my feet, and I just didn't know what to do. When I got over the shock that she didn't come when I called her I began walking around our block and asking if people had seen her. So many people had spotted her, but I couldn't see her and it was no response when you called her. I feared so much seeing David because I knew he loved that dog like it was a child. I headed back to the house and kept myself busy packing. When David arrived home he kissed me and his next words, "Where is Dee?" I explained to him in detail what had happened. I could see the sadness in his face. He went to the front porch and sat down and called Dee's name off and on for one hour. That is all we talked about that evening and just wondered where she was. The routine of David coming home each evening and calling for Dee continued until we packed the U-Haul truck to move to Daytona Beach, Florida. I was excited and forgot about being sad.

Moving day came and several of our close friends came by to say goodbye. David drove the truck and I followed him in our little brown Omni full of all our green plants. We drove non-stop to Atlanta. Experiencing Monteagle, Tennessee, was absolutely breath-taking. Everyone should experience going over that mountain; it is simply wonderful. Upon arriving in Atlanta we checked into our hotel. After eating dinner and relaxing a bit I called my first cousin Kevin, who came to the hotel to visit us. We had a wonderful visit, kind of catching up on the family news and happenings. He is the only male cousin I have that is exactly my age. As the visit ended I told him to keep in touch, and he agreed. The next morning came and we headed out for the expressway once again. The land was flat and not as exhilarating as Tennessee. I love to travel, so the highway is like home to me.

As we arrived in Daytona Beach, Florida, following the map for directions to Bethune Cookman College, we carefully navigated ourselves right to the campus. Once on campus, David stopped and asked a student for the location of the Music Building. The student rode over with David and parked us directly on the parking lot. After freshening up and locking the doors of the car we entered the Music Building, a nice new building with lots of space. Hearing music from the choir we entered in. Dr. Rachel Wells was directing the choir. When she saw David, a big smile came over her face. She continued to direct, however. Once the song ended she hugged David and asked him if he had a good trip and asked him if he brought his wife. He looked around for me, and I had slipped into a seat next to one of the students. As he pointed me out Dr. Wells remarked, "She looks like one of the students." I knew from that one comment the lady was pretty powerful. They talked briefly and then we left to go to a hotel.

The next morning, we contacted a real estate office who had found a house we could rent in Ormond Beach, Florida. Ormond Beach was full of retirees and money, and it was seven miles from Daytona Beach. As the Realtor showed us the two-bedroom, one-level stucco home it was just perfect. He said to us that he hoped we would be okay because he had never sold or rented to a black family in this area. We liked it, so in we moved. Our neighbors to the right were nosy seniors, our neighbors on the left overly friendly. That new address was 1909 Myrtle Jo Drive. We had well water so the electric bill was all we had to pay. The back yard was big with lots of shade trees. The garden lizards were running everywhere so I knew I would be in the house most of the time. The stove was harvest gold but we had to furnish our own refrigerator. We used the money the church had given us and paid for our U-Haul and the new harvest gold refrigerator. As we moved in, it did not take us long to get everything in place. Dr. Wells came to our home and made the comment that no one on her staff had ever lived in Ormond Beach. I knew by that comment we had moved far enough away from the campus and activities. I had worked all the time in Nashville so David told me to relax and don't worry about a job. We met another music instructor and her family and planned a weekend trip to Disney World. I had so much fun that day. It was good to be out of school and not working. I felt on top of the world. After leaving Disney World we were so tired but not so tired to not roll in the sheets. We loved a lot and long after, and then fell fast asleep. We woke up to a beautiful sun shiny day and headed for the beach. There were lots of others who had the same plan. The waves and hearing the sound was most refreshing and calming. Watching the cars drive on the beach, and watching all the people, was much excitement in our new surroundings. We both loved the beach.

After about two weeks of staying home and seeing David off to work each day and periodically talking to him throughout the day, I was bored with the routine. I began to seek employment. Dr. Wells told me I could interview for a nutrition professorship at the college. Saul Morris, a former church member, told us over dinner before we left Nashville to never depend on income coming from the same institution because they could fold and no one would have the needed resources to keep going. Once in the interview all was going well until they began to try and figure out where the money would come from to pay my salary. I whispered to God, "If you allow me to leave from these people I would find my own job." Sure enough, the next morning there was an advertisement for a chief clinical dietitian at Ormond Beach Memorial Hospital.

As I arrived at Ormond Beach Hospital it was quite impressive. The palm trees lined the driveway and the flowers were breath-taking. I entered the building and went to personnel. I was interviewed by Mr. John Smith. He was a nice man with a strong Southern accent. At the end of the interview he offered me thirteen thousand dollars per year and asked if I could began working in two weeks. I was replacing a pregnant dietitian. I left with the job in my hand and it was just good to know that in just two short weeks I would be working again. I had worked all my life, so working was just a part of me.

I began working the middle of September and had made one paycheck before David received a check. I couldn't help but think about what Saul Morris's advice had been. We had been accustomed to being broke, so getting two checks, we thought we were rich. As we settled into our new surroundings we found ourselves longing for Nashville. We would whine to each other about Nashville, and then we would call our friends and talk for hours about missing everyone. Settling down, I found a wonderful female gynecologist, Dr. Kim Wang. Dr. Wang removed my intra-uterine device and gave me a clean bill of health. Since the birth control was gone, we began to think about having a baby. It seemed strange but I had promised David upon completion of the Ph.D. and my dietitian license we would work on having a baby. Every other week David would take urine samples by the doctor's office. After three trips and David saying, "I know you're pregnant," and, "I can tell because your hips are getting wider," we had a positive pregnancy test. David was excited and called his parents right away. I told him he would have to tell my dad. I was having flashback of when my dad would tell me if my sister or I ever get pregnant we would have to go back to where we got pregnant. Back then, I couldn't picture myself anywhere but at home in my own room in my own bed.

The next day after the positive pregnancy test David called the doctor's office and asked when the baby was due and the nurse replied, "Sir, you will have to bring your wife in." The nurses made a joke about it in the office, so when we came in for the initial prenatal visit, they teased David about that question. I really had mixed feelings about being pregnant. I didn't feel physically different at all but I just wasn't sure mentally.

In October 1980 we went to our college homecoming. Our friends and relatives were so glad to see us. Returning home for college homecoming was just a family tradition. If you didn't come home at that time you just missed a great gathering of African Americans everywhere for an entire week. We didn't tell people that we were expecting a baby. It was too early to tell. After the football game on Saturday I went to visit my first cousin Emma Jean. Emma's husband opened the door for me and led me to the bedroom where she was in bed. Emma was forty-five, and she was my wild cousin who would say anything. We laughed and exchanged stories and then when it was time to leave she pulled the cover back to get out of the bed and to my great surprise she was pregnant. I asked her screaming, "Girl, how did you get like that?" And she said, "You know." I was in total shock seeing her pregnant and then I began to laugh, and I told her I was pregnant too. We came to find out that our children would be different in age only from February to June. After the laughter and shock, we hugged and kissed, so I went back to Mom and Dad's house.

David would always hang out with his friends at homecoming so I got myself ready for bed knowing it would be late when he returned. When he came in I heard him moving around and I woke up to talk to him. He got in bed and told me everybody he had seen. Then he wrapped his body around mine and began to become horny. We kissed and petted heavily and I told him we had to wait until we got back to Florida. "I can't have sex in my parents' house, plus they may hear us," I said. We laughed and were soon fast asleep.

Morning came and the big rush was on to get up get dressed and get downstairs for breakfast and leave for church. We always went to church while we were at home. My parents expected it. The morning breakfast prayer was always special. We all said in unison the Lord's Prayer. The chant was mumbled and words not pronounced and all mixed up. It was all I could do to keep from laughing out loud. When we ended my dad would sit and say a Bible verse then everyone else would follow with their verse. My sister always said, "For in thee O Lord do I put my trust," so I learned to say the same thing also. Everyone did this each Sunday morning before breakfast. The breakfast always consisted of waffles, scrambled eggs, bacon, sausage toast, and plum jelly. When breakfast was finished we gathered in the car and went to church. Our friends and especially our minister were glad to see us. The church service was always inspiring, and the deacons always began the service by calling and lining hymns. This was a tradition before service really began. It was always good to see Dr. Doc Wiley, our church organist, and our former choir director Shelby McPhee. We were their students, and they were proud that we were both employed successfully. After church the hugs and kisses from old friends were always welcomed. On the ride back to my parents' home my mom would fill us in on the gossip of the church people. Most of the stuff was pretty disgusting to hear about church folk. Once at home, Mom had a Sunday dinner spread of homemade rolls, chicken, beef roast, green peas, corn, salad, pound cake, and peach cobbler and so we ate until we were hurting.

After helping Mom clean up the kitchen we began to pack.

Mom always had fresh canned foods, and Daddy had potatoes both sweet and white. I brought an extra-large suitcase with me just to pack my foods in it. My brother James came by as we were loading the car to go to the airport. He started to pick up my food suitcase and he couldn't lift it off the ground. It took two men to put that suitcase in the car. Honey, it was no way I was leaving my food in Arkansas.

After returning to Florida and arriving in our driveway we noticed the roof of our neighbor's home was filled with egg shells, and the tree wrapped in toilet paper. We wondered what had been done to our home and everything was quiet and in place. We knew each day that we were the only blacks in the neighborhood, and we stayed inside mostly.

Back at work on Monday, people were asking me about my trip and I told them it was super and that I had all my food for the winter. They looked at me in amazement. Most people are used to living close to home so they can stop by their parents' home or go by Momma's house and get a fresh home-cooked meal anytime. Since I couldn't do that, I transported my food, canned and frozen. They couldn't believe my frozen foods remained frozen the whole flight. I wasn't worried about their belief. I knew I had home-cooked food for the winter, and I was too very happy.

The monthly visits to the doctor's office were quite boring. My stomach was not sticking out. Only my breasts had enlarged, and my butt was huge. David asked the doctor, "Well, she's six months, when will her stomach show signs of being pregnant?" The doctor assured him it wouldn't be long and that I was carrying the baby in my hips. We listened to the baby's heartbeat each visit, and it was quite strong. The nurse always asked a long list of problems and she would check "no" to all. I would always sit in her chair saying, "no, no, no." My pregnancy was most uneventful. I was healthy, happy, and had little weight gain, no swelling and no pains. I carried out my normal duties as usual. I always carried raisins, carrots, apples, and crackers with me because I would get hungry all of a sudden. No morning sickness ever.

David had thrown up most mornings in October and November, and I had taken him to the doctor thinking his ulcers were acting up. We came to find out he was having my morning sickness. He also would come home and go right to sleep because he would be so tired. This went on for months. Bless his heart; it was almost like he was pregnant too. He was quite a bit overweight, so while I was pregnant he gave up red meat of all kinds and lost weight.

There were many days of working and leaving work and heading for the beach. We would often walk on the beach right after work. It was relaxing and refreshing. Spring surely brought a new picture, and by late April I began to wear maternity clothes. I remember one of the older cafeteria employees saying, "Honey, I can't believe you are pregnant. I can usually tell by the breathing up and down at the base of the neck and collar bone and plus by the color of your neck. Honey, your neck didn't even get black." I smiled because I had read in a book that due to the increase of hormones during pregnancy among women of color, the pigmentation of the body would change, the neck being most noticeable, because the face would usually remain the same pigmentation. Little did she know I was rubbing facial esoterica on my neck evenings and mornings. My hair was growing, and I was a beautiful pregnant woman.

Attending Lamaze class was quite helpful. Our classes were every Thursday evening at Halifax Hospital from 7:00 P.M. to 8:00 P.M., where I would deliver the baby. When we would go, each class would focus on a different subject. The class on anesthesia was extremely stressful for me. I realized we had started something and to get out of it would be quite painful and it couldn't be helped. The instructor explained spinal, put to sleep, epidural, and natural methods of anesthesia. No way sounded good, so I chose natural and began to prepare myself for a natural delivery. No needles for me. While the instructor was explaining the different methods, I began to cry. David looked at me and said, "Are you crying, but why?" And I said, "It's going to hurt, and it's no way out." He held my hand and rubbed my back and kissed my tears away.

David had made friends with several students and faculty. Bryan James was one of David's closest friends. He visited us quite often, and they hung out together late, often near the end of the pregnancy. On one particular visit he made the statement that I sure was getting big. I smiled. Bryan was an artist and worked and displayed his work at the Volusia County Art Center. He always talked loudly, liked to eat, and was very intelligent.

May came on, and I was in full bloom. I could not put my pantyhose on by myself anymore. This was quite frustrating for me because I am an independent person. David would help me each morning and he would say, "Come on, baby, let me help you put your pantyhose on." Just having him say that made me want to holler. David would always tell me he would help me wash the dishes, so I decided not to wash them anymore. Dishes had piled up in the sink for three days. David always involved himself with students, so on this evening with three days of dishes in the sink he tells me he was having the students from the fraternity over to our house for dinner. I realized no women were attending so I went to the bedroom at 5:00 P.M. and went to sleep, not helping wash one dish.

The students came and I woke to their noises around 8:30 P.M. I was so hungry but I knew David was angry with me and I knew I didn't want to dress to go out in front of all those guys. On my night stand sat a bottle of vitamin C chewable tablets. I must have eaten the full bottle, and they were large. That helped a little, and then the hunger returned. I heard someone go to the restroom so I cracked the door and it was a student named Tim. I told him to tell David to come to the bedroom. When he came I asked him to bring me a plate of food. He never did so I ate the whole bottle of vitamin C and went to sleep. I woke up at 1:00 A.M.

The house was quiet, and David was asleep. I got up and fixed toast, eggs, and fruit, and drank milk. I finally got to eat. I realized from that experience David taught me to not depend on him to help with the housework. He always found something else to do after meals. Maybe only clearing the table, but never washing dishes.

Working, working, and people pampering me at work was beginning to get on my nerves. Every step I took someone was asking me either how I was feeling or when was the baby due. David called me one day at work, and I was so frustrated I didn't make patient rounds that day. He told me to cheer up. We were leaving for the graduation in Nashville so it would give me a few days' break. I almost forgot our trip.

Days before the trip, I was so excited and nervous about flying three weeks before my due date. I just kept my nervousness to myself, careful not to worry David. Packing my clothes for the trip, I was so careful because I wanted to make sure I was looking good.

The day came and we caught our evening flight. When entering the plane, the stewardess looked at me as if to say, "Where are you going flying this pregnant?" I smiled and got in my seat and put my seat belt on. David settled in his seat and began to read a newspaper. We had a smooth departure. Once in the air the baby began to move a lot. David looked at me and said, "Are you okay? You look so afraid." And at that moment he began to pass out and his body was flexing and jerking. I asked if the stewardess would please bring some orange juice. David was having a hypoglycemic attack. Seeing him like this was just the beginning of seeing lots of things. Once he drank the orange juice he questioned me about what had happened to him, and I explained. He was surprised. David told me he had not eaten all day and that he had smoked a joint before coming home.

Joint smoking was his favorite pastime but he did not smoke around me often. This habit was always shared with Bryan or someone else he met who liked smoking joints. He smoked while we were in college and I just thought it would go away once we graduated college. David never stopped. The joint smoking made him happy, relaxed, and hungry. I could always tell when he was high. This was a daily habit. Often I would ask him to stop and he would say, "I'm not addicted to it because I only smoke once or twice a day."

The "Fasten Seat Belt" sign came on, and we were in Nashville. Our good friends Derrick and Candice Trout picked us up from the airport. We spent Thursday night with them. On the way from the airport Candice and I caught up on the latest happenings in Nashville. As we were on our way to their house they said, "Let's stop by the church." We got out of the car and went in to speak to old friends. To my surprise the Fellowship Hall was set up for a surprise baby shower for me, and the people there had been invited. I was overjoyed. I received diapers, bibs, nukes, towels, socks, pins, etc. It was simply a wonderful gesture. That night I told Candice I could hardly sleep because I was so excited.

The next morning we were up early. David's parents, James and Susie Walker, came in from Memphis to attend the graduation. There were many students graduating from Vanderbilt in May 1981. David had completed all his requirements in August 1980, but Vanderbilt only had one graduation ceremony per year. David had received his cap and gown in the mail, and I had pressed it the night before. After finding seats, the ceremony began. When they called for the Ph.D.s and called David's name, I was so proud because I had walked with him through the tough times and good times. I knew I could tease him and say it's my Ph.D. too, and he would smile back and call me Mrs. Dr. David L. Walker. On this day we seemed to be closer than ever. I guess with the new baby coming, my being a registered dietitian, and his graduating from Vanderbilt was a sure sign that we had worked together and accomplished much. I had tears of joy because I remembered the days we didn't have much food to eat. I remembered the days it was so little gas in the car we had to choose where we would drive for the day. Just remembering we had come past all that together made the day worth the wait.

After the graduation we got in the car with my in-laws and headed to Memphis to visit relatives. Anytime we came to town Susie would invite everyone over to see us. Susie would cook and feed the whole community. David's boyhood home was a two-bedroom cottage with one bath, living room, and kitchen. Recall that my father-in-law was a loan shark; people were always coming and going. You always had to keep your clothes on because people would even come in the bedroom to speak to us. After everyone had visited, David asked if I wanted to ride over with him to see Ronald Jackson, one of our college class-mates. I told him no and that I needed to rest. He left and my mother-in-law and I cleaned the kitchen up and got into bed. At approximately 1:30 P.M., my father-in-law came in saying, "Get up, bitch, get up, I'm going to cut your damn head off." Susie said, "James, what do you want me to do?" He just continued to yell, "Get up, bitch." I peeped into their room and Susie told James, "James, you know Deborah will hear you talking loud. James, please be quiet." He said, "Hell, I don't care who is here." I wanted to help her so bad, but I knew with me pregnant and if he hurt me, David would kill him. After my thoughts passed, I heard him snoring. I thought, "He is drunk, now he is asleep." I came out and asked Susie if she was okay. She apolo-gized for me having to overhear him. I hugged her and told her it's okay and I got into bed. When David returned I explained to him what happened. That morning he told his dad he would not bring his family to visit if he could not control himself. He did apologize to me.

After the discussion we loaded the car and headed for Pine Bluff. I lay down in the back seat of the car all the way home. I was so tired from all the excitement. When we arrived in Pine Bluff my mom and dad were glad to see us. My brothers James and Matthew teased me about being so big. Matthew kept telling me to let him see the baby move, and my six-year-old niece Catherine kept saying, "I want to see that baby." My dad said, "See, you got that child looking for a baby that can't be seen yet." We all laughed.

That night when it was time to go to bed, I went into mom's bedroom so she could see my stomach. She told me I looked good, that I didn't have many stretch marks, and that my color was good. We laughed and while I was dressing I asked her, "Now you're still coming to stay with me for three weeks?" And she said, "Yes." I knew I would need the help of a woman after delivering the baby, and I sure knew it would have to be my mom. If you remember the TV show *Hazel*, my mom was just like her. She was clean, organized, and just plain good woman who knows how to run the household. I just couldn't do without her. I slept in bed with my mom that night. We must have laughed and giggled until we fell asleep. Up early the next day before it was time to get on the road, I was sorry our time was so short at home, but everybody wanted to see me pregnant with my first baby. Loading the car was many hugs and kisses. I told Dad, "Remember, Mom has to come to Florida when the baby comes." He said "Okay" with a smile. This trip Mom told me she would bring food when she came since we had to travel back to Memphis, plus I had all that baby shower stuff from Nashville. Driving away from them this time seemed hard, and I guess it was because I wanted to spend more time at home.

I lay down on the back seat all the way back to Memphis. When we arrived, Papa Jack, David's grandfather, was sitting on the porch with David's father and Susie. When we drove up, Susie asked if we wanted something to eat, and we said yes. Susie always had a lot of food cooked, and her kitchen had food and was greasy all the time. Susie was a good soul food cook but was definitely not a good housekeeper. My father-in-law placed moth balls in the candy bowls, closets, and the refrigerator. You always smelled of moth balls when you left their house. Often when visiting, my sinuses would give me a fit. I just couldn't understand the moth balls. Papa Jack told David to be good to me because "when a woman has a baby for you she really loves you." He told us if the baby was a girl, name her Mary and if it was a boy, name him John. I just smiled at his suggestions because I knew I didn't want a Junior. Saying "Junior, come here" sounded so country, and it didn't allow the individual to be an individual. James and Susie took us to the airport after saying goodbye to Papa Jack. After boarding the plane, I thought, "Now if we can just make it to Florida without having this baby I will be happy." We both slept on the plane back to Florida. The baby jumped one good time and frightened me. I didn't close my eyes again.

On the ground, back in Daytona Beach, Florida, I was so happy, I had made my traveling rounds without any incidents. At home that night we talked and fell asleep. Sleeping was beginning to be hard for me because the baby was larger and moving around a lot. I slept with lots of pillows. Back at work it was the same with people asking me how I was and how much longer I would work. The patients I had while I was doing rounds would purchase gifts for me. I received so many flowers and gifts that my administrator asked me not to accept them because I was an employee. I told him if a sick patient in bed was giving me a gift I would have to accept it because they went through a lot trouble to get the gift for me in the first place. He was quiet and said a few more things and I was back to my office.

There was a VIP suite in the hospital, and rich people already filled the hospital but the VIP suite was for the super rich. As chief clinical dietitian it was my duty to take an order from the VIPs for things they wanted in their refrigerator and the kinds of snacks to be stacked in the cabinets. I hated doing this because it made you feel like a maid. Plus to top that, one of the VIPs was a little old, old, rich white man who thought I was dirt poor and grew up hard, and he wanted to know how I made it through. After several conversations we became good friends. Upon his discharge all the administrators had to escort him out of the hospital to his waiting limousine. The director of the hospital was talking to him and asked, "What was the best thing that happened to you in the hospital?" And he came back real strong, "That little black dietitian girl." I was too shocked. They all looked at me strangely, and I smiled. As we walked away the director said, "Mrs. Walker, you have a way with the patients. Good work! Public relations is important." At home that night I shared with David what had happened. Of course he already had heard days before about this man.

On May 31, 1981, David was invited to do a full concert in Jacksonville, Florida, at a Baptist church. Bryan James accompanied us on this trip and Lillie Crane, pianist. Jacksonville is about a forty-five-minute drive from Daytona Beach. The baby was resting on my bladder so we had to stop a lot for me to go to the bathroom. I had never seen Bryan so quiet. He was afraid I was going to have that baby right there in the car. He kept asking, "Are you okay?" I smiled and said, "It's okay, man." The concert was a great success. David's lyric tenor voice was well received by all. At the reception afterwards so many people shook our hands and asked when I was due. I had fun replying, "Anytime now, anytime." The trip back was just as stressful for Bryan. When we got back to our house he laughed and said, "I've never been so glad to see your house as I am right now." We laughed as he drove away.

The Blessing of Children

It was another morning fighting to put pantyhose on. I was so tired, and it's Wednesday. I thought, "If I can just make it till Friday then I can be off." June 3 started like most days. Pantyhose struggle, David saying, "Come on, baby," eating breakfast, being dropped off at work with a kiss because we only had one car. At work I was so tired, and my thigh muscles kept hurting. When making the morning rounds I told an R.N. She said you probably need to be off your feet. By lunchtime I just wanted to sleep but my legs kept on hurting. I sat in the office that afternoon. By 2:00 P.M. I called David and asked him to come and pick me up and maybe we could stop by the doctor's office on the way home. By the time he arrived everyone in my office was saying to him that I just needed some rest. Dr. Rome Hendrix was a wonderful doctor. We had no appointment; we just stopped by. Dr. Hendrix examined me and told us to pick up a suitcase from home and go straight to the hospital.

We left the office with my pantyhose in one hand and shoes in the other. David was ahead of me telling everyone, "We're having the baby today." At home I called Mom and Dad, and David called James and Susie. Both sets of grandparents were too excited. Off the phone, I took a shower and then tidied the house up a bit. After getting the suitcase together we got into the car. On the way to the hospital we stopped at Woolco. We both got out of the car to shop for the camera. My thighs were in great pain but I didn't want to sit. The lady at the counter was very kind and helpful. She asked when the baby was due, and I told her we were on the way to the hospital. Once she heard this she became too nervous and another sales clerk had to help us. The new sales clerk was calm and even took a picture of us in the store and gave it to us. After purchasing a camera, we were back in the car. A train pulled onto the track so we had to wait even longer to reach the hospital, finally arriving at the hospital at 5:30 P.M. An attendant waiting with the wheelchair said, "We've been expecting you since Dr. Hendrix's office called at 3:00 P.M. and said you were on your way. I told him we had to tidy up the house, bathe, stop at the store, and he laughed while pushing me toward the elevator. David caught up and they put us in the labor room. When the nurse checked me she said I had dilated to eight centimeters. I told them I didn't want an IV, and they said we will check with the doctor. Dr. Hendrix ordered it, but I told them they would have to let me walk because my thighs were hurting bad. As I walked David sang different spirituals to me. He was nervous but trying not to show it. I was in pain but trying to be good through it all. He sang and I walked with my rolling IV while the nurses came in and out and smiled. I told David I needed to go to the bathroom and the nurse said, "No, no, let me check you." This time when I lay on the stretcher she said the head was crowning. She gave David his blue scrubs and told him to get dressed quickly. I was saying, "David, don't leave me, please don't leave me." The nurse was saying, "It's okay; he'll be right back." When he returned I was rushed to delivery. Once inside everyone was yelling, "Don't push; let the doctor get his scrubs on." All I could remember during that pain was the Lamaze instructor saying once the head is out the pain will be gone. So I began pushing. David was at my face and shoulders and was also saying, "Don't push." When he saw me close my eyes tight and grit my teeth he knew I had tuned everybody out. He kept calling my name and then he slapped me. My eyes flew open and there was no more pushing. At that time Dr. Hendrix said, "I'm pushing the baby's head back in to do the episiotomy." Once he cut, the baby's head was out and then the shoulders and behind (7:37 P.M.) And he said, "You have a boy weighing eight pounds and twenty-one inches long." I looked at his little wrinkled body and face and said, "Look what we did." David was laughing, and our nurse was taking pictures because we forgot all about the camera. After my clean-up in delivery, David walked our new baby boy to the nursery. I caught a chill so they put lots of warm blankets on me. After napping off and on in recovery, I was moved to my room. David had called the grandparents and other friends and told them we were fine. Visiting hours had ended, and they were asking David to leave. I told him, "Be sure you call me when you get home."

Once at home he called and I could tell he was sleepy so we said good night. He had kissed me so much before he left the hospital, I told him, "Not another baby now." He smiled. After hanging up the phone the door flew open and there was this little tiny framed black lady rolling the bassinet in. It was time for the baby's first feeding. The little old lady said, "Honey, you breastfeeding?" And I said "Yes, ma'am. "She said, "Put your nursing bra on and don't take it off. Now you don't want your breast to sag or you'll be heading further South before you want to." She was very firm, serious and no smiles. She put the baby to the breast, and he knew what to do. I looked at him in that moment and thought, "My very own son, a baby, me?" I thanked God and then I kissed my son for the first time. It was truly a special moment. The nurse returned and took the baby back to the nursery. In the middle of the night just a few hours later he was back for another feeding. By this time I was feeling tired from the night before, and I was so sleepy. David arrived with roses, cards, and balloons and a big smile. When the baby finished nursing, we began to try and decide on a name for him. We remembered the names Papa Jack had given us. We thought, "No Junior." But we both wanted the baby to have a part of his dad's name so we named him David Jon Walker. We named him David after his father, David L., and Jon after his great-grandfather's suggestion. We were both pleased with the names, and they sounded real solid. I completed the birth certificate information and the nurse picked up all the papers. It was feeding time again.

During the pregnancy I studied breastfeeding so much. My grandmother had eighteen children and breastfed all of them. She would tell me that the reason children are so crazy today was because they were drinking cow's milk. She told me that the breast milk is the best because it comes with the baby. After hearing all her stories I just couldn't feed any other way. One night while watching *20/20,* an ABC special, there was a whole story on the dangers of commercial formulas. It showed the formulas lacking in several key nutrients causing the children to have deformities they didn't have at birth. After seeing that, I said no one is going to come up to me and tell me one of my child's legs is shorter than the other or his brain is half-developed due to the formula. Breastfeeding is the best no matter what.

All day my phone was ringing with congratulations and we had many visitors who came and said, "We looked for your baby in the nursery but we couldn't tell him from the white babies." David Jon was red and bald. We would laugh. I told them, "He is easy to tell because he is the largest among the whites, and they are always rocking and holding him." I could hardly wait for evening to come because Mom was flying in. I took a shower when David left to pick Mom up from the airport. I knew if I waited she would tell me that I couldn't bathe for a whole week; it was old folks' tradition. I figured I better shower and dress before she came. When Mom arrived, the baby was in the room. She scrubbed so she could hold him. The nurse would hardly let you in the room at certain times because the hospital had very strict policies about company and baby contact. She pulled the blanket back and looked all over him, and said, "He sure is a big red one and just look at the slick head." She gave me a real big hug. I realized then that I was second to that grandbaby. We talked and David teased her about being a grandmother. He and my mom had a special relationship due to the fact that he was the only son-in-law. My mom always told him, "David, you are my favorite son-in-law," and he would laugh and say, "Yes, because I am the only son-in-law." After visiting me for a while they went home for dinner. I knew Mom would unpack her things and begin cleaning my house. David returned to the hospital and talked about the good dinner Mom had prepared. David sat on the bed and hugged and kissed me and told me how lonely he was sleeping in the bed all by himself. I smiled and said, "I'll be home before long. It's good for us to miss each other; it makes our hearts grow fonder." We talked a little while longer, the baby came for his feeding, and David left for the night.

The next morning came with several mixed emotions. It was time to go home. I had a wonderful pregnancy and delivery and I felt I would sure be an okay mom but I was nervous about taking my oh-so-small baby boy into the great big world. My sister had arrived the night before and had stopped by the hospital to drop off his going-home suit. She had flown in from Washington, D.C., and would be here a couple of days. She came back early that morning and wrote all the information in my baby books. She has excellent penmanship. They brought David Jon in for me to dress so after they took him to the nursery and took those famous first pictures then it was time to go home. I wore my pink and white flowered dress with elastic in the waist home. Mom had sown it for me. My stomach had gone down so much that people were saying, "You don't even look like you've had a baby." I would smile because I made sure I ate all the correct nutritious foods during pregnancy, and it didn't allow me to gain a lot of unnecessary weight. After I packed all our things, the wheelchair came in and David was so happy to take his new addition home. Inside the car I thought every car going down the street was going to hit our car. I couldn't wait to get into the driveway. Mom was watching as we drove up.

When I walked in my home it was clean as a whistle and inside the bedroom awaited a whole new set of mattresses. My mom told David that they had to shop for new mattresses and they must be delivered before I came home. I was surprised. I hugged and kissed David for the new mattresses. He later said, "Girl, I paid six hundred dollars for the set," and said my mom insisted. I was glad. I just smiled at his comment and said, "You get to sleep on three hundred dollars and I get to sleep on three hundred dollars each night. Now that should equal a good night sleep." After putting everything away and getting settled there at home, Mom pampered me for three weeks. My sister washed my hair and curled it, and my mom had a fit. She said, "Girl, you're going to catch cold." We made sure we dried it well and I wore a scarf over the rollers. It felt so good to have a clean scalp. I had many guests that day. David was in and out running errands and then Bryan came by. David told him he was the godfather and I remained quiet, because I wasn't quite sure about Bryan.

The first night at home with the baby, I didn't know what to expect. Mom put me to bed early. David Jon woke up at 11:00 P.M. I hit David and told him to turn the light on and he did. I changed the baby's diaper and I sat up to feed him. He went fast asleep. When he fell asleep I hit David again and I said, "Turn the light off" and he did. David Jon woke up at 2:00 A.M., I hit David and told him to turn the light on and he did. I changed the baby's diaper and I sat up to feed him. He then wanted to play, thinking it was day. After about forty-five minutes he went fast asleep. When he fell asleep I hit David and told him to turn the light off and he did. It was 2:45 A.M. When I woke up for the day it was 7:00 A.M. I looked into the bassinet, and the baby was gone. I hit David and said, "Where is our baby?" And he asked, "What baby?" I jumped up. Becoming more awake and realizing he wasn't in the bassinet I went in to ask Mom. There was David Jon wrapped tight in his blankets. Mom said he woke up around 5:30 and cried and cried. She said she heard him and realized I was so tired I slept right through the 5:30 A.M. feeding. That was my last time sleeping all night. When I asked how she got him to go back to sleep she said, "I wrapped the blanket around him tight just like they had done in the hospital nursery and he fell asleep." She said, "Girl, I knew you were tired." Coming back into the bedroom David asked where was he and I told him what Mom said. He reached out to take him while I sat on the bed.

Sunday afternoon came and our minister and his wife from the church we attended came by. We sat and talked. They really made on over the baby. While sitting there I began to have hard pains in my legs all over again. The pain was so great I had to excuse myself to the bedroom. Mom came in and asked if I was all right. I told her about the pain. She gave me Tylenol and left me to rest. After resting a bit the pains subsided.

The nightly routine began again to bed early. David Jon woke up at 11:00 P.M. I hit David and told him to turn the light on and he did. I changed the baby's diaper and I sat up to feed him. Again he wanted to play thinking it was day. After one hour he went fast asleep. When he fell asleep I hit David and told him to turn the light off. At that moment he got up and went to the bathroom. When he came back he came on my side of the bed and said, "See, look, you have the same lamp on your side of the bed as I have on mine." He began to turn it off and on. He said, "See, it's working. I don't have to wake up for feeding," he laughed, "because I just checked it." We laughed. The next morning I heard him telling a couple who were friends of ours talking to the husband, "Man, let your wife breastfeed because my son doesn't cry at night and you can sleep through the night." He laughed and continued talking.

Breastfeeding was quite a challenge. Few people were breastfeeding, and you couldn't get a voice of experience. Grandma Cassie was deceased so she couldn't help me. In talking with Mom she told me to call Janita who was my first cousin's wife and had successfully nursed their daughter, and she offered lots of encouragement to me. Just talking to her over the phone made me feel a bit easier about the decision I had made to breastfeed. You would be surprised how my experience from breastfeeding built my character. I remember so many days of praying, "Lord, please increase my milk and give me the strength to do all the things I need to do." I reminded him that I was a new mom and trying to continue my role as a wife and find myself. As time went by I became a pro-breastfeeding mom.

My mom offered so much support. David Jon was a difficult baby to burp, so when my dad would call asking when she was coming home she would say, "I can't leave yet because they haven't learned to burp the baby. I've got to keep working with them."

As my strength returned and I recovered we went shopping a little. People would stop the stroller just to take a peek at the baby. David and Mom talked about going to Disney World. We were only forty-five minutes away and she would be leaving soon. The next morning we packed and headed for Orlando. We checked in the Ramada Inn and off they went, just Mom and David. They wouldn't let me go because they said the baby was too young so we stayed in the room and slept most of the time. They came in for dinner and I told them I was glad they remembered me. They knew I wanted to have fun with them. After dinner they returned to the park for the parade and fireworks show. After returning for the night David said, "Girl, I am tired. Your mom had us riding everything, even Space Mountain." He said he nearly died. He seemed to be happy about the overall day they'd had, and so was she.

A few days before it was time for Mom to return to Arkansas we took lots of pictures so she could show them off once at home. I felt wonderful and it was all because my mom had truly taken care of me. She took care so much so that David kept asking her to stay. After a quick drive over to the beach, we took Mom to the airport. I called Dad and he was glad to hear she was returning home. I told him thanks for letting her come; David thanked him also.

We were on our own. I was okay for a few days after Mom left, but all of a sudden I would cry and couldn't stop. David called my mom and told her what was happening, and she said I would be all right, just adjusting to all the responsibilities. When I was crying in my mind I was wondering, "Can I be three people at once? A wife, a Mom, and find me?" The days were full with lots of things to do. I just began to pray for strength, and soon those frequent tears were no more. I picked my crying self up and said, "It's me. Let's press forward." I did with the strength of the almighty God.

We had a week between my mom leaving and my mother–in–law coming. They had called every day to ask about the baby. My mother-in-law arrived, and I had it all back together. Getting myself together then was to my advantage because my mother-in-law was wrapped up into cooking for her son and holding her grandson. David was the only child born between James and Susie. He had two older brothers that were by his father and a sister, whom my mother-in-law never thought was his, so we didn't see much of her. For my mother-in-law this was her first. She was obsessed with her son, and he was the apple of her eye. She said David weighed nine pounds at birth and she breastfed him for six months. She would tell us that she nursed at her mother's breast until she was four years old.

My mother-in-law was so different a person than women that I was accustomed to. She dressed flashy, cursed, stayed up all night, drank alcohol, talked about all the violence in the newspaper and on TV, gossiped about family members, and loved to tell tall tales and laugh. David had shared with me the relationship he and his mother had. She was a cosmetologist on Beale Street in Memphis. She worked all day and into the wee hours of the morning. It brought in excellent income but long hours away from home. David spent long hours in the shop and was exposed to all kinds of life issues early. People were naturally crazy about him because it took his mom a long time to conceive him. Everyone referred to him as "our baby." He was special not only to her but others as well. Still he stayed up and out all night also.

Her visits were mostly spent catching him up on what was going on in Memphis. We did a lot of sightseeing. David's father would call and ask about everyone. Susie always asked him who had called her for the day. David went to a meeting in New York for a week, and my mother-in-law and I were left alone. I was nervous, but I wasn't, all at the same time. We talked mostly about breastfeeding, the family back home, etc. One evening we made a trip to the grocery store and upon putting the groceries in the car, she noticed a liquor store next door. She asked if we could go, and I told her it was fine. Once inside she made her selection. As we were leaving she said, "If James knew I had this baby in the liquor store he would kill me." I was quiet. We returned home because she had her nightly shows she liked to watch. I never saw the alcohol bottle again.

One of my friends called me and invited us over for dinner. As we sat and talked, my mother-in-law participated very little in the conversation. I kept noticing her watching the clock on the wall and looking at her wrist watch. After observing this, I felt we should leave. On the way home she told me my friend was nice and the dinner was good. When we turned in the driveway she said, "Lord, child, I thought I was in Memphis and I kept thinking I need to get home before James does." If she wasn't in when he arrived he would keep up a lot of drama. Once the shop was moved next to the family home due to urban renewal, he would be most upset. She apologized and sat quietly, then she said, "He's got me crazy."

David returned and as always when he went on trips he brought me a gift back. He bought back two dresses that really fit my body. After being home a couple days it was time for Susie to leave. She had cooked greens and spinach and we put them in the freezer. We drove her to the airport and she told us she would call us as soon as she got home.

David Jon was growing quite fast, and I was getting used to being a mom and wife. I had to self-talk because I didn't have a lot of people around me who would encourage me. At our six weeks' check-up David Jon had gained four pounds and I had lost twenty pounds. My doctor told me to eat, and I told him I was and he said that continuing to take prenatal vitamins throughout breastfeeding would be good for me and the baby.

David came home from work one day and smiled and asked,

"How would you like to live in Little Rock, Arkansas?" I said, "If that is where you want to be it's okay with me." Dr. Wells saw that David was talented so she gave his name to Dr. Robert Mudson, president of Philander Smith College. Philander Smith was a small United Methodist-supported college. David would be applying for director of choral music. We talked about moving and in the back of my mind I was glad because it would be close to Pine Bluff (my hometown). My thoughts about being happy were destroyed when he said, "Now we are not going to go to Pine Bluff often just because we are closer." I thought to myself, "This is really selfish." I never made a comment. I called my parents and told them we would be coming home in July so David could interview at the college.

Packing for myself and the new baby was hard with trying to make sure I had everything. We flew into Little Rock and picked up a rental car. David went to his interview while I visited relatives in Little Rock. After his interview he said it was quite successful and they offered him eighteen thousand dollars per year. This amount was good because he was only making $13,500.00 at Bethune Cookman. He was very happy.

We left for Pine Bluff and spent the weekend with my parents. This was Daddy's first time to see his first grandson. When he held him up to look at him and talk to him, David Jon had a huge smile on his face. I told Daddy, "He's never smiled that big at any one," and Daddy said, "The boy finally sees somebody that looks like him, bald." We laughed. My brother, my sister-in-law, and my precious nieces came in. Everyone took turns holding the new baby. Catherine, the younger niece, had to be watched closely because she was jealous of the new baby. She was six years old and had been the baby grandchild all that time. Venus and Nicole were older and they were just glad I was home because they knew they would get to spend the night with us and that we would do fun things. I loved those nieces. My dad and David talked about the move and when we would have to be here. He was pleased to know we would be closer, and so were David's parents. Mom was really glad because my grandmother Julia was in the nursing home in Little Rock. Mom could always spend nights with us when she came to visit grandmother Julia. I was so happy inside and I could hardly wait for David to accept. I kept my joy to myself and didn't share it with him because I remembered his comment in Florida before we went to the interview.

The next day, all of our cousins, aunts, and uncles came so they could see the new baby. They all had so many questions from how I was feeding him to when we were going to start him on baby food. He had been held so much that when it was time to go to sleep he was so fretful. I just rubbed his back and held him close. He soon went to sleep. David knew several of his old friends who were still in Pine Bluff so he went to hang out with them. After getting the baby to sleep, my nieces and I talked to my mom and caught up on family happenings. We talked so long that David Jon woke up for his feeding. I fell asleep in Mom's bed, and we just slept there for the night until the next feeding. When he woke up again, I got up and moved upstairs to the bed with David.

The next morning we were busy getting packed to return to Florida. Daddy was busy getting some bar-b-que out of the freezer for me to take back. I was so glad to get that bar-b-que chicken. When you are homesick it's nothing like eating Daddy's bar-b-que to get you well. Anytime I got homesick I would eat that bar-b-que chicken. Mom hugged and kissed us goodbye as well as Daddy. I told them we might see them real soon. They smiled. Upon returning the car to the airport in Little Rock we boarded the plane. David Jon fell fast asleep, and so did I.

Back in Florida, David continued to go over the pros and cons of moving. I had already begun to pack because when he said he wanted to do something, really it was pretty much done. He asked me one day what were the boxes for and I told him "I'm packing," and he laughed. He said, "Girl, you think you know me." and I said, "Yes, I do." A couple of days went by and he said, "I've decided to take the job in Little Rock," and I said, "See, I've got my packing almost done." When he called his parents about his decision to move, they were so happy that my father-in-law paid for the moving van. We took the southern route to move. Still being new parents, we were looking at the baby while slowing up at a red light and bumped the car in front of us. There was no damage, but "Silly us," we thought. I didn't get to do much long-distance driving. David Jon would wake up for a feeding more often when I was driving, and David said it was a conspiracy to keep him driving most of the way.

Arriving in Memphis, Susie had the usual family crowd. Lavonia, T.J., her friends. When we got out of the car Susie took the baby up and down the street to show all the neighbors. When she returned, James fussed at her because the neighbors were seeing the baby before he was. He got David Jon and held him until it was time to feed him. My father-in-law said to David Jon, "Boy, go on so you can get some of that litter jug." I had never heard this term used before for nursing. It was so vulgar sounding to me. My mother-in-law referred to it as my "titty." I thought about how country and backward their comments were. These comments would go on and on then I would just leave the room.

That evening I went to bed early with the baby. David was up talking to his family and then he later went out to see friends. That night James was quiet and so was Susie. There was no loud talking or threatening to fight. David came in and slipped into bed on one of the night feedings. We talked about his visiting old classmates and soon fell asleep.

The next day we were headed to Little Rock. We found an apartment on Wolfe Street that was near the college. It had two bedrooms, living room, bath, family room, eat-in kitchen, basement, and closed-in garage. David told me that all he wanted me to do was to stay at home and keep the baby. We didn't have any bills so I committed to being a stay-at-home mom. The movers came and I began to unpack and get things settled between feedings. David Jon was three months now and nursing every two to three hours. It just depended on him and his little schedule (that could never be depended on). In about a week, everything was in place. When David began working, I would get up at 5:30 A.M., feed the baby, bathe him, and put him back to sleep. I would wash up and then get David up for work. While he was getting dressed I was preparing his breakfast. We would sit and talk and then he was off to work.

Every evening when he came home, the baby and I would be dressed and ready to go and he would say, "I'm too tired." Sometimes if he fell asleep I would just take the car and go out with the baby. I only knew people he introduced me to and I didn't like not having my own friends. Everyday was the same routine. Then a sudden change happened one Friday when David came in around 11:00 P.M. He had not called. This went on for the next month. I decided that something had to be done so I thought, "I'll stay dressed keep the baby dressed and we will go into the basement and when he comes in, I'll come in two hours after him." When you're in the basement you can hear every footstep. When I heard the garage door go up I put my coat on and carried the baby with me to the basement. I heard him come in and go straight to the bathroom, then he went to the bedroom. When he noticed we weren't there he went to the family room and turned the television on. It was midnight. At 2:00 A.M. I opened the door to the garage and eased into the garage while pushing the opener and the door came up then I pushed the bottom and the door came down. When I opened the door at the bottom of the steps to go up to the main floor David stood there. He was so nice opening the door for the baby and me. Once settled he looked at me and asked me where I had been and I told him, "Oh, I didn't ask you where you've been on all these Friday nights." I told him, "I just decided to go out since you decided not to call or come home on Fridays anymore. I had fun where I was, and I might be going out every Friday night also." He was so quiet and I was laughing on the inside because I had been at home all night. He never once thought about what I could really do with a breastfeeding baby out all night. Honey, honey, honey, my scheme worked. That next Friday he was home at 4:00 P.M. We went to dinner and a movie. We had a wonderful evening. Periodically he would ask, "Where were you that night?" And I would tell him, "You can't be out there and at home too. You're only one person and I'm only one person and I haven't asked you where you were." He volunteered to tell me that he was with the boys, but I never told him where I was. (Smile.)

Just before the Christmas break, David got word from work that each faculty member would have to take a pay cut of fifteen percent to help keep the college open. All faculties agreed. By then I was so tired of being a stay-at-home mom, day in day out. I got up one morning, dressed, and told David I was going to look for a job and if I didn't find one, I was moving to Memphis with his parents.

Mrs. Lindsey the babysitter was a wonderful loving lady whom my aunt introduced me to. She kept David Jon for the day. I went out and I interviewed for nutrition administrator of the state Area Office for Aging. They hired me on the spot for fifteen thousand dollars per year. When I went by to tell David he said, "Girl, you always get a job in one day." I smiled. He took me by to pick up David Jon, and Mrs. Lindsey agreed to keep him every day while I worked. I went to work the middle of January. I really enjoyed going on the site visits and seeing the senior citizens at mealtimes. Senior citizens were always special to me because I had spent so much time with them. I began to meet friends, and working was so rewarding. My check came in handy since David had gotten a pay cut. We only had one car so I was taken to work and picked up from work. I didn't mind because it allowed us to spend time together. Things were going super at the college for David with numerous concerts and TV commercial opportunities. We were always busy attending college functions after work. I always kept David Jon with us no matter what we attended. They just got used to seeing him. I never let too many people hold him because he would be too hard to fall asleep at night so he was mostly with me or his dad but he was with us. By spring we had joined Mt. Pleasant Baptist Church. The people were friendly, and we felt right at home. We attended Sunday School, and this was quite different for David because he never went. I grew up in Sunday School and loved the Lord. David in Sunday School had a lot of questions for the teacher. You could tell he needed to study. We came each Sunday, and it was always interesting. David joined the choir and sang whenever he could.

The college choir would travel on many weekends raising money for the college. Some weekends I would go to Pine Bluff and visit my parents. David had made friends with several people. He had a friend named Toby who was his weed provider. I don't care where we were, weed would follow. Toby would call often asking to be taken to the store or Wendy's most often or to the laundry mat. He never came into our home, just to the door. He was always dirty-looking and unkempt. I always asked David why he kept company with him and he would say, "We're just smoking weed together and hanging out. It helps me to unwind." I kept quiet. Many times I would write David letters if I didn't feel comfortable putting it in verbal terms, and I thought the letters were useful also because he could read back over what I said if he needed to. There were many letters because he forgot what I needed with the baby, the housework, and just having a family night. We were always going but going around others, mainly friends of his. I knew that the baby and housework were left to me. He would play with David Jon while I cleaned.

One Sunday while looking in the classified section I noticed a job opening for a surgical dietitian at Doctor's Hospital. I thought this job would allow me to be closer to home since I had to do day travel with the State Nutrition Aging job. I applied for the job at Doctor's Hospital. Delilah Upchurch interviewed me for the job. She was from Ghana, Africa, and had married an African American. She had a heavy accent but seemed very friendly. After a week she called me and told me that if I wanted the job it was mine. I started out making eighteen thousand dollars a year. This was wonderful, and we could sure use it. My grandmother always told us to keep our money together; that way if one person made more money than the other it would not be a problem as long as everyone was sharing out of the same account. David seemed happy about the new job. I worked 8:00 A.M. to 4:30 P.M., so these were good hours for the baby, too. My job was quite interesting, and I was learning so much. One dietitian I worked with graduated with me from college and two dietetic assistants had also graduated with me. The working atmosphere was quite friendly, professional, and educational. Most of my patients were gastric bypass patients, knee and hip replacements, stomach stapling, acute care, general surgery, and the like. My patients were quite ill. Most of them were on clear liquids, blended diets, soft diets, to TPN, etc. Each day was a new challenge.

Every morning when we came into work it was customary to meet in Delilah's office for morning prayer. I really liked this idea because being a new mom and continuing my role as a wife had its challenges. I had never really prayed out loud in front of other people before, so this was the beginning of strengthening my prayer life. We would all pray for each other's patients, family members, children, and spouses. Delilah and Azalea, a nurse secretary, were true prayer warriors. You could tell that they had been praying a long time. They told me to always lay hands on David Jon and pray for him. I began to practice this, and it worked. I even began to pray for others away from work. My friend Susan Cole, in Memphis, called one night totally excited. She said she had been saved and she could speak in tongues and she wanted to share Jesus with us. What she was saying was so overwhelming that it didn't seem real. She was extremely excited. After talking with Susan on different occasions, I began to read my Bible more but still not a whole lot. I knew I was living right so I felt that was good for right now and we were in Sunday school each Sunday and church each Sunday. Scripture memorization was just not on top of the list. Delilah kept me praying mornings and talking about God throughout the day. My life was being surrounded by strong Christian women, and I was learning so much. One time Delilah told me she had gone to this church and the minister had laid hands on her and she was slain in the spirit. All she remembered when she woke up was that they were brushing grass from her hair. I remember her inviting me to go with her and I said no because I was thinking in my mind, "I don't want them to brush grass from my hair and I not know where or how it got there." She invited me so many times, and I finally agreed to go.

This night I had my guard up and I was watching as the minister touched people and they would lay them on the floor. He laid his hand on my head and I remember saying in my mind, "Don't fall, don't fall." I didn't fall, but a warm feeling was present in my body. He asked the congregation to go and find someone to pray with. An older white lady came and took me by both hands. Her voice was so soft and sweet. She began to pray for me in general and then in the middle of her prayer she spoke, "My daughter, I have seen all the tears you've shed and I've heard all the prayers you've prayed." Then she began to pray for my parents, my brothers, and my sister, and then she thanked God and ended her prayer. I could not believe what I had just heard but I knew I had heard it for myself. After service I looked for the lady but I couldn't find her anywhere. I wanted so badly to ask her why she said my daughter and I wanted to know how she knew I had been praying and praying especially for my parents and siblings. When I couldn't get the questions answered I knew it was God.

At home that night I was excited and told David about my spiritual experience. Afterwards I told him to kneel and pray with me. I had never prayed out loud with him before so when the prayer ended he called me a "Holy Roller." It was clear to me after his comment that I was growing spiritually and he was not going along with me. After his comment I would not pray out loud before him again. I remembered back in Iowa that he told me he had been called to preach around December of that year. He told me that he had talked to the Reverend Franklin Jones and he told him that it was a high calling and that he must be sure. He pondered much but didn't acknowledge it publicly.

David's job was going well and the students loved him and our whole family. Toby, the unkempt guy, was in the background. It was like a cloud that wouldn't go away. One evening when we drove up to the garage, the garage door was up. I asked, "David, did you leave the door open?" He couldn't remember. The door leading into the house was shut. When we got out of the car and went into the house, we knew our home had been burglarized. As we approached the front door it had been kicked in. Things were thrown everywhere. Mattresses off beds, clothes on the floor, and the refrigerator open. Our stereos, TVs, and David Jon's bow dollar pig bank was among the missing items. That is a sick feeling when you know someone has been in your house and taken your things. The police suggested an alarm. We called Rollins and were set up the next day. I guessed inside that it may have been Toby and some dope-smoking buddies who had done this awful thing. David was quiet and didn't place blame anywhere.

Back at the hospital my job was going well. I had met many people and I was settling in. Dr. Richard Bryer was a family practice physician whom I met one day in the hospital. All the nurses said he was a wonderful doctor and had a thriving practice. I chose him as our family physician. We went to Dr. Bryer for David Jon's shots and physicals, my general examination, and David's exams. We could all see Dr. Bryer.

A patient was admitted to the hospital from an old nursing home facility. On the outside of the door a sign was posted warning that this patient had scabies. Instructions and precautions were listed so I followed the procedures on the door to the letter. This was a difficult patient due to age, dialysis, treatments, heart problems, and hypertensive condition. The diet was hard to develop because there were so many things this patient didn't like to eat and if she did like it, she couldn't eat it anyway due to the potassium and sodium content. After a long day at work and this patient was long discharged, I came home and played with the baby, cooked dinner, and watched TV. I got up to go to the bathroom and I remember all day my pubic hairs seemed to be itching . I had that feeling so I decided to take a close look. As I moved my pubic hairs apart there were these tiny little bugs all over my pubic area. I called for David and showed him what was on me and then he checked himself. They were on him also. I began to cry and cry because I didn't know what it was. I called Dr. Bryer and he told me to come in first thing in the morning to be examined. David and I both went in and he told us it was scabies. I told him about the patient I had in the hospital and he was just quiet. He gave us a prescription for the body soap and he made it clear that both of us had to be treated. I was still breastfeeding the baby and I asked about him. He said the baby is fine, just treat yourselves. I cried over and over and over and David was so patient with me and he hugged me and said that it was okay and that we would be fine after a few days. He showed his love so much during this time period.

David Jon was growing and learning so much. He was a real easy baby to wean from the breast because he would play so hard. June was here, and David Jon celebrated his first birthday with all his friends from Mrs. Lindsey's house and his church friends and others I had met in various places. We always made birthdays really special around our home.

David Jon began school at the Sixth Avenue School in downtown Little Rock. It was near the college so it was easy for David to drop him off each day. Later we moved him to the Winfield School due to smaller enrollment and more individualized attention. He was receiving excellent pre-school instruction, and my mom was working with him also. We knew he was gifted. He was actually reading words at eighteen months to two years of age.

David would be out late most evenings at the college or rehearsal. He would always be home for dinner. Sometimes we would be asleep when he came in. When he came in late he would slip into bed with me, play around and then get up and read or grade papers. He was a night person. I woke up one night to hearing David Jon and David singing. I got up and told David, "He's got to get his sleep. He can't be a night hawk like you." After that, David would read in the living room so David Jon wouldn't know anyone was up.

We enjoyed going out to eat, and David just liked to eat food, period. He loved fried chicken, macaroni and cheese, peach cobbler, pound cake, and donuts. I always tried to keep my weight down and I would struggle most of the time going up and down. I always exercised and enjoyed walking mostly. David would exercise every now and then. He was not big on physical stuff, outside work, or washing cars. He was all "Mr. Clean Professor."

One evening as we sat and watched TV, I noticed David was going to the restroom and urinating a lot. He was feeling weak also and had signs of being thirsty and weight loss. I told him we need to go and see Dr. Bryer. The next day we saw him and he was already treating David for high blood pressure that he'd had since age fifteen along with stomach ulcers and diabetes. He told him that it could be controlled if he lost weight and followed a diabetic calorie-restricted diet. At home I prepared the foods for him, and he stayed the course. The blood sugar was being controlled with medication and diet.

I saw Dr. Bryer just a few months earlier so he could remove my IUD in plans for our second child. We had tried for months with little success. I thought our schedule was too busy. After an examination by Dr. Bryer, he told me my uterus was tilted. He explained in order for me to conceive we would have to try different positions. I hated the penis being placed into the vagina from the back but that worked. I finally conceived, and our second child was due to be born June 26, 1984. After trying so hard not to have children born in the same month we didn't quite make it. We had a September conception again.

David's choir was growing more and more popular. We were traveling on the weekend or attending different activities. Being pregnant meant nothing to me. I did the same work and kept all my same activities. I asked the nurses at the hospital whom they would recommend as a good gynecologist/obstetrical doctor. Everyone referred me to Dr. Rex Catcher. He was a young physician with a super personality. I made an appointment to see him, and I made an appointment with Dr. Bryer for David to see him because he was going through his morning sickness. I could tell I was pregnant easily this time by watching David's behavior.

My pregnancy was uneventful just as the last. When I went to Dr. Catcher, the nurse would ask sixty questions and I would answer "no" to all of them. I ate just like I did when I was pregnant before because I knew just what to expect this time.

While in prayer one morning before work I told them I was pregnant and then three months later Cathy, another dietitian whom I graduated from college with, announced she was pregnant. This was her second child, too. Cathy and I ate lunch most days together and enjoyed each other's company since we had so many things in common. Delilah and Azalea said they were not going to drink the water because of our pregnancies. Delilah would pray so hard for our pregnancies to go smoothly and for our children to be blessed. All I knew was having a second child wasn't quite as exciting as the first. It just seemed like a longer waiting period.

Things began to go crazy in our lives all of a sudden. Ashley, our landlord, sold the home we were living in so we had to begin looking for someplace else to live. I remember falling on my knees crying and sobbing and telling God to please help us to find a new location. I just had a feeling that we had been in Little Rock and it would be soon time to move anyway, but it was just a feeling. Each day after work and on weekends we would look at places to buy or rent. It was a tiring process but it had to be done. We liked living in the city and knew we didn't want to live way out and we still had only one car. We drove through the Qua-Paw Quarters quite often because this was the city's historical district. It was a quite charming area. The governor's mansion was located there, and Will Minton was the governor of Arkansas at the time. Each weekend we would look and one weekend we located a house that was gutted on 20th Avenue. My father and brother came and looked at the structure and told us it was a good house but it needed lots of work. We purchased the house for twenty-two thousand dollars and got a home remodeling company to bring it up to standards. There was a lot of selecting to do so we met with them and told them what we wanted. We had the hardwood floors refinished, a new bathroom, a new kitchen, air conditioning, roofing, and painting throughout. Our backyard was shady and shared the governor's mansion fence. We didn't realize we would see the governor, Will Minton, jogging most days. The company promised to complete all work on our new home within six weeks. In the meantime, we had to move sooner than we thought because a buyer bought the home where we were living. We pondered moving to Pine Bluff with my parents and commuting daily or getting into an apartment. None sounded good.

Sunday morning came and I was so glad to begin worship. My weeks were draining with the pregnancy, normal activities, and locating another place to live. We had met a wonderful family in the church named Bill and Jackie King. Bill was an internal medicine physician and Jackie was a social worker. They had purchased a home in the Qua-Paw Quarters and had renovated their home. Their home was huge with lots of rooms and space. I observed them at church most Sundays. They had four teenagers, and those teenagers were always hugging them and stayed close to their parents all the time. That was a sure sign that they were great parents. At the close of worship Jackie came over to me and asked how everything was going. I explained to her all the things we were going through. At the end of our conversation she invited us to live with them until they finished our home. This was a sure blessing because their house was just four blocks from the house we were renovating. This would allow us to go by and check each day on the progress of the renovation. It was close to everything and nowhere from the college. Being close to the college was important because David would go back and forth a lot.

A few days before we were scheduled to move David got very sick. He was urinating a lot and was dehydrated. I called Dr. Bryer and he told me to bring him to Doctor's Hospital. Once there, Dr. Bryer told him that if he ate right and exercised he could go without insulin. The timing of this hospital visit was quite out of sync. On moving day, I ended up having to move our things that I had packed by myself to the detached garage of the home being renovated. Then I had to move our bedroom furniture to the King's home, and I was seven months pregnant. My mother-in-law came and sat in the hospital with David. She laughed when I told her that he picked a good time to get sick while I'm half-pregnant and having to move. She couldn't figure out the half-pregnant part. We just laughed. Upon discharge the plan was to follow the diet and exercise. We arrived at the Kings's. The family was glad to see him. We had our own private quarters, and we retired upstairs for the evening. Living with the family was quite interesting. There was typical running here and there and questions about who was fixing dinner and what was for dinner. We only saw them when it was time to eat or leave the house. Daniel and Lisa, the fourteen year old, loved to aggravate David Jon. He wanted to play but I had to keep him with me due to the trauma he would experience sometimes trying to play with them. To them he was just a toy. We always made sure we stayed out of the family's usual activities.

We wanted to live as if we weren't there (kind of invisible). Sometimes in the evenings I would come in and wash the dishes and clean the house. Jackie fussed at me about this because she said her children had their assigned chores and I was helping some and not others. Jackie enjoyed walking so we would go to the track of the neighborhood high school and walk. I would tell her, "Maybe I can walk this baby out before May so it won't be a June baby." She would just laugh at me.

As the weeks grew closer for our renovation to be complete I was so happy just to know it would be just our family once again and David Jon wouldn't have to worry about the occasional trauma. They were not quite finished when we decided to leave the Kings's home. They told us we needed to stay another week but we told them we had imposed on their family long enough. They understood. My parents and the King family helped us to move and hang curtains. I was eight months pregnant by the time we settled into the house. I had lots of help moving in because everyone knew the baby was due soon. I continued to work every day at Doctor's Hospital. Everyone was teasing me because I was getting so large. I felt fine but I was just plain tired of being pregnant. The second time around was so boring. Because I was still walking with Jackie, I figured I was in good shape and I knew that would help during my labor. After walking, David and David Jon would be playing. David Jon would ride his tricycle all throughout the house. The rooms seemed to connect and he would somehow manage to make all the connections. He was a busy child and was always getting into things. He was so happy and would say the funniest things. It was never a dull moment with him around. The hospital offered brother/sister sibling classes and we attended. They showed the children the nursery, they gave them a gift to give to the new baby, and then they gave the child a gift. We always talked about the baby coming because we wanted him to be prepared. I knew it would end our time as mother and son alone, but I knew we would both adjust. Each night David would rub my back, and the pantyhose scene returned. David really enjoyed teasing me about not being able to put on my pantyhose.

David Jon's third birthday came on a Saturday. We invited all his usual friends. McDonald's was the place for the party. It was a great place for a child's party because they provided the entertainment, the food, and the clean-up. You get to go home and feel rested. Once again to work and April seemed to be moving so slowly. By the following Friday I was so ready to leave work. I was just tired. My feet were swelling each evening, and this never happened with David Jon. I mostly lay around all day Saturday. Saturday night I began to have a few pains but I could sleep through them. Sunday morning I got up early to get breakfast ready before going to Sunday School. Just before we left, I took one last trip to the bathroom and noticed my mucus plug had passed. I changed my panties and went to Sunday School. Once in church service I told David to begin to time the contractions. He remained calm. When church was over people were saying, "I thought you would have had the baby by now," and I told them, "It is going to come before the day is over." They would smile as if I were kidding. Mrs. Cottonham, our pastor's wife, was asking how I was doing. I told her that David was timing the contractions and that we were on our way to pick up my suitcase and then to the hospital. On the way home from church we stopped at Woolco to buy a camera. We just couldn't have a solid camera in place and around for these deliveries. Once at home I called Linda Barrett, a dear friend, who came over to stay with David Jon while I delivered. I called Mom and she said she was on her way. I had told Linda to hurry and she did. By the time she arrived I was feeling a lot of pressure on my bottom. I told David when getting into the car to step on it. (3:00 P.M.) We parked the car and walked to the elevator. When the door opened there stood Dr. Catcher. Once inside he said, "Mrs. Walker, you're making me miss the basketball game and I just don't believe you're in labor because you're too calm." David said, "You don't know; she's ready. She was quiet with her last pregnancy." He smiled and we were on the delivery floor as the elevator door opened. Once on the examination table he said, "You're at eight centimeters but your water has not broken. If I break your water the baby will come sooner." All the nurses standing around kept looking at me through the contractions. They could not understand why I was not screaming or hollering.

I had not eaten since breakfast, and I felt so weak. As I began to feel more pressure on my bottom they pushed me into the delivery room. The nurses were still staring, watching the monitor and watching me. When they told me to push I was only closing my eyes tight. Dr. Catcher kept saying, "If you just push I can get back to my basketball game." I was too weak. On one push David raised me up from the back and it helped a little. They let me rest as the doctor checked. He said, "If you can just push hard one good time, the head will come." I did as he said. I told him, "Please stretch the vagina lips so I won't have to get stitches." He went around the lips and the head came out but the hips tore me so I had to get only two stitches. It was better than the seven stitches I got with David Jon. He announced that we had a baby girl. The first thing David said was, "Isn't she precious?" I thought, "We only have a boy's name picked out." I was nervous about a baby girl because I was used to the boy and I just knew it would be a boy. She had a full head of hair. She was born at 3:37 P.M. weighing eight pounds and thirteen ounces, and was twenty-one inches long. Dr. Catcher told me, "You know, I teach medical students and I could have filmed you as a model had I known you would be so calm." My husband told him, "I told you she knows when it's time."

I began to call people in the food service office. They said they would send me a good dinner. I told them that I needed it because I was hungry. I called Linda back at the house with David Jon and she was excited. My mom came in while I was telling David Jon about the new baby. Mom took the phone and said, "Girl, you had that baby before I could get here." It only took thirty-seven minutes. By 4:00 P.M. I was in my room. I called Mrs. Cottonham, our pastor's wife, and she couldn't believe I had the baby that soon after church. I told her to tell everyone hello at night service and asked her to think of some girl names. I had named the baby I carried for nine months Daniel Nahum. In our family we all have biblical names. Visitors came offering so many different names. Delilah? Oh, no, that just did not sound right. In the meantime as we were thinking about names, Mom and David Jon came up to my room. I hugged and kissed him and he seemed to wonder why I was in the bed. Mom hugged and kissed me as we were always glad to see each other. The nurses and doctors from all over the hospital were coming to see me. Mom said, "I'll be glad when you get to come home so you can get rest." I was in the hospital for three days. So many gifts and visitors came in. I had at least a three-month supply of diapers before I left the hospital.

It took us the entire three days to name the baby. She was called Baby D until we decided. We named her Dannelle Felecia because Dannelle is a derivative of Daniel and Felecia is my middle name. I remember a minister saying naming a child is so important. The child needs to feel connected to family and know what the name means as they carry the name for the rest of their lives. So we had a biblical name and my middle name. We completed the birth certificate and were discharged from the hospital. I didn't have the same feeling riding in the car with Dannelle that I did with David Jon. I felt no one would hit our car and I had grown so much in the Lord. I felt very relaxed.

At home adjusting to two children was a little challenging. Because David Jon had spent so much time with his dad and grandmother when I arrived home he would go the other way. When I noticed this, I knew I would have to work to get him back to me. It was as if he said, "How dare you bring the baby into our space!" Often I would call him over to hold or help me with the baby. This seemed to work as the days went by. After two days at home, he wet his pants. David gave him two switch licks on his little legs and he never tried to wet like the baby again. Putting him to bed was a problem also. I put him in bed and he cried and screamed, "You make me mad, Mommy!" over and over. I went in and got the switch, two licks on the leg, and told him, "Only dogs get mad and you're no dog." I patted him on the back and he dropped off to sleep. There were no more problems after that. Mom was angry because I spanked him. She kept telling me I was going to hurt myself spanking him so soon after delivery, but he was my child and I knew I needed to get his attention back before she left me alone with the children. Little by little he realized his place was still intact.

By the weekend Mom and David Jon would leave for Pine Bluff on Friday evening and return to Little Rock on Sunday evening. She would leave my meals prepared and everything else would be done also. I only had to care for Dannelle. You talk about a woman blessing a woman. My mom was just the greatest help. She helped with all the chores but didn't handle the baby. I wish every woman delivering a baby could come home to a woman like my mom. You didn't know she was in the home most of the time because she worked so quietly. She kept David Jon busy. Her years of teaching school came in handy with her only grandson.

Unlike after the delivery before, I stayed at home in pajamas all day. I didn't want to go out. I would get up shower and put my robe on. After six weeks I was still in my robe and inside all day. David thought I was having postpartum depression. I was so comfortable inside. I knew I needed this down time because once I began my activities again, they would not stop. Most women only get to rest after a baby, and it's no rest then because you have to work with the baby. During my seventh week, my mom came and brought my three nieces to stay with me. Yes, I had five children, but believe it or not, it was easier than taking care of one. They all helped each other and all I did was feed and bathe Dannelle and comb my nieces' hair. They would dress themselves, the baby, and David Jon while I cooked or took a shower. David was out of town for a conference, and they were good company.

When David returned he asked Jackie to come over and talk to me about being in my robe. I told Jackie, "I'm fine." I said to her, "I know my husband, and we will be running here and there very soon." Two days later he said Dr. Ronald Sampson, chairman of the music department of Tennessee State University, called and asked if he would apply for the vocal music professor at the university. It would be a ten thousand dollar increase and such a great opportunity. He was excited. I had mixed feelings and told him we just settled into this house and having the support of my family would be sorely missed. After praying about it, we decided to move. I moved with no job and I just trusted God to help me find a job if it was in his will. Just as I had told Jackie I would be on the move, I was. Packing was all left up to me. Moving back was welcomed because we had good friends in Nashville so it didn't feel strange. My family was sad but I said, "I've got to follow my husband," and they understood. Once in Nashville we moved to Buchanan Street, which was a small two-bedroom dollhouse. We were still paying a house note in Little Rock, rent in Nashville, and still I had no job. Things were tight financially. The house we were in was so small. Every day I would sit and cry because I had never lived in such a small space. I tried not to cry in front of David because I didn't want him to feel that he was making this all a bad situation because we moved. But I would cry. He assured me that it wouldn't be like this always and would kiss me all over my face. We returned to Nashville in August 1984.

In October I had to fly home, Dannelle and I, due to the passing of Grandmother Julia. Many attended the funeral and they were all glad to get to see the new baby. David and David Jon stayed behind. David tried to get David Jon on the plane trip also because it was university homecoming and he wanted to participate in all the activities without a little one hanging around. After I returned my girlfriend Candice told me David and Derrick stayed out all night and had left David Jon with her and she was asleep and didn't know he was in her house until morning. I felt so bad but I was mad at David for not taking care of David Jon the entire time I was gone. Whenever I got mad at him I always wrote him a letter if I felt I couldn't put it to words. He would sit and read my letters carefully and responded positively afterwards. He knew whenever I wrote him it was serious and I would be looking for change, not the same old same old.

Before I left for Arkansas, I had applied for a state Women's, Infants, and Children's nutritionist and dietitian at Parkview Hospital. The position at Parkview was a tray line dietitian checking the special diets, and it offered very little income. The state job was part-time so I took it because I was still breastfeeding Dannelle. I traveled three days a week to different places close by to continue to work. When I accepted the job and realized we only had one car and I needed to travel, I thought, "We've got to have a second car." We got up early on Saturday morning and went to Hansen Chrysler and looked at several small cars. We finally decided on a red Plymouth Horizon. When the salesman handed me the key I hugged David, then I hugged the salesman. The salesman replied, "I wish all my customers were this happy when they bought a new car." I knew this ended years of waiting and waiting. It was the beginning of picking up your keys and your car always being in the driveway for you. I was so happy. The days I traveled were so relaxing. It gave me a time away from the family, and once I returned I would be ready to work. Dannelle was growing quite fast and was a good baby. She was a little partial to me but it was okay because she was my baby girl. She was a happy baby who sometimes screamed so much that Alaina Timothy (friend) predicted she would be a singer. She would say over and over, "That baby is going to sing because she screams too loud."

Working the Women's, Infants, and Children's Supplemental Food Program was such a rewarding experience. I was able to help advise so many other moms by literature and from my wisdom. God had blessed me with a gift of encouraging and helping others to breastfeed without giving up. I just loved those moms. All the people I worked with were wonderful people and I looked forward to my travel the days I worked. I began to carry my Bible to work with me and I would sit quietly and read passages while waiting on another client. I missed Delilah and the prayer group so much and I was longing for that relationship again.

In the spring David took a job as minister of music at Spruce Street Baptist Church. They had a very active children's ministry so I involved David Jon in it. David Jon was also attending Head Pre-school before starting the university pre-school. I went on field trips and volunteered on my days off work. I was happy working part-time but soon became tired of the travel.

My children caught chicken-pox. Those chicken-pox lasted six weeks so I had to resign from my job. Chicken pox has got to be the worst disease a child could go through. Those pus-filled bumps make you not want to touch your child at all. It's awful. Once over the chicken-pox, I began to apply for another job. I really enjoyed being with my children. By now it was almost birthday time again. It was time for Dannelle to turn one year old. It was hard to believe my baby was turning a year old. Dannelle was such a precious little baby. Mom made all her clothes and I kept her dressed up all the time. It was always easy to dress David Jon because he wore mostly pants and shirts.

Once again I found myself as an employee. I took a part-time job with Maury County Hospital as a relief clinical dietitian. I would travel to Columbia, Tennessee, on Thursday and Friday. Columbia was a small, quiet town with some growth. The people were very friendly and made you feel at home. After being there for a couple of weeks, they asked if I could move my whole family from Nashville to Columbia. I explained to them that my husband was a big-city person and was very happy with his job and that I knew we would not be moving. One day when I showed up for work on my desk sat a clipping from the newspaper announcing a position as choral music director at the local community college. I laughed and said to myself, "These people are serious about me moving here with my family." I took the announcement to David and he laughed also. Once we finished laughing we got on a serious note and said, "Now let's think of someone who would need a job." David thought about Quincy Easton, a home friend and college classmate. David gave Quincy a call and he was happy to hear from us. Quincy came for the interview and got the job. This was too funny to me because shortly after he moved to Columbia I took a job in Nashville at Cloverbottom Developmental Center in August 1985. Quincy, however, would visit us quite often because he liked the city, too.

Working at Cloverbottom was certainly a new experience for me. It took a while for me to get used to the physical disabilities of the patients there. I did a lot of self-talk and soon seeing all the disabled patients didn't bother me anymore. This job had many challenges. Because of the kind of patients I had, I had to read, study, and figure out different formulas for the different conditions. The physical setting was so peaceful. I would walk from cottage to cottage to see patients. This was always a welcomed time. There was no phone and no one calling for Mrs. Walker; it was simply peace. The whole atmosphere was peaceful and slow-paced. This job was like none I had previously occupied. The people in the kitchen were quite comical and led lives very different from mine. I was careful only to eat fresh fruit because the salad maker would stir the coleslaw with her arms and hands and some of the male cooks had engine oil underneath their nails. The bake shoppe was quite different. Mrs. Luca ran it and she was a clean cook. Every time she baked rolls she would come and get me out of my office. I would eat two rolls for sure, then three, and after that I would stop counting. Cinnamon rolls, cornbread, ooh-wee, just good eating. It's a wonder I didn't weigh five hundred pounds just from eating Mrs. Luca's rolls and baked goods. A lot of days I would have to schedule myself seeing the residents during roll-baking time just to avoid Mrs. Luca inviting me to the bake area. It's strange but she never left any baked items on my desk for me when I returned.

The men would always woo at me, and I would tell them I am happily married. One guy, Coy, was crazy. Every day he would say, "Quit yo man for me and I'll make you happy." I told him he needed to spend time being a husband to his wife and a father to his children. He started talking to a white married lady in the kitchen who had a family. Bridgette and Coy would have sex in the vacant cafeteria on blankets. After becoming pregnant, everyone wanted to know whom the baby would come out looking like since Bridgette was sleeping with a white male, her husband, and a black male, her lover. When she had the baby people couldn't wait to see that baby. I was even curious. Those who came back from visiting her in the hospital said, "Mrs. Walker, that little boy is golden brown." So it was Coy's son. Bridgette told her husband the baby was brown because he had Latino in his family. She was so proud of that baby. When she brought him to the kitchen, Coy took him and showed him to everybody. Once alone with Bridgette, I asked if she would eventually tell the baby who his father really was. She said no because she slept with her husband every night and she was not leaving him because he lived with her during the entire pregnancy. All I could think about was that they would have mixed-up lives forever.

Then there was Daddy Banks who, if anybody said anything to me, would always get them straightened out. He knew I had home training and had been cared for and not run over by a lot of men so he protected me and highly respected me. Then there was Mr. Jakes, who was a redneck from the heart, with no morals and no values. He was just a loose man. He dated a young girl in the kitchen and rumor had it that Brittany's husband was going to shoot him one day. One morning I came in really early as they were running the breakfast trays. Mr. Jakes,

Brittany, and other employees were standing at the wheeled carts serving breakfast. All of a sudden a shot rang out. Everybody on the line was down on the floor. I'm sure everyone thought Brittany's husband had shot Mr. Jakes, but it was a blow-out from the steam table wheel. They teased for months about him being down on the floor. If you ever got bored all you would have to do is go to the kitchen and boredom would end.

While working with the residents I met a wonderful Christian woman, Valeria Gables. Valeria was married and was about the same age as I. My son and her son were born in the same year. We would walk early in the morning before work and exchange stories. I had never opened up and talked to a female the way I talked to Valeria. She was real personable and seemed to be able to keep things to herself. She was not one to spread your business all over town. Her son had been born with a disability, and she would share that story with me often. She also talked about her parents and her brother who was living out of the will of God. I began to share my family stories and how I was struggling with trying to be wife, mom, career woman, and find myself. It was then after five years of marriage that I began to ask myself and Valeria, "Why do I need a husband if I have to do everything for everybody?" She said to me, "This is the way it is," and from what she could tell and me, too, most women in our lives had lived through and gone through much more than we ever had. At one point I was thinking of divorce because I was tired of being left to care for the children, left to pay all the bills, cook all the meals, and clean the house. I was fed up. It was then that Valeria told me to just pray for strength. I had already been doing that but it became daily and habit-forming. Those things I was focusing on became small issues, and I just pressed forward because I loved my family even though I was carrying the load. I never wanted to divorce. I was just tired of having to do it all, and that was not a good-enough excuse to divorce. Valeria had the same feelings and shared them with an older woman so that was how she was able to encourage me. Each day we prayed for strength and for our families. Our friendship became very close. We didn't talk on the phone after work or on weekends. We were true walking partners and enjoyed it.

Attending church each Sunday at Spruce Street was good. The children were very active in children's activities, and I worked wherever I could. If you were not a member, your activities were limited. I thought churches would allow you to participate in activities and then you join because of feeling comfortable, but this church had it backwards. The members were crazy over David Jon and Dannelle. I always made them sit quietly and would discipline them if they didn't. They knew how to act in public and at home. Each day I would pick them up from school and daycare. I would have the radio blasting and I would sing whatever was on the radio. One day I was singing Michael Jackson's song, "Girl I Want your body, gotta gotta to have your body" and the spirit said to me, "What are you singing, what are you saying?" I turned the station to another station. I believe it was WPLN public radio. When I picked the children up they were so full of chatter that they never noticed a new station. As time passed one day when we got in the car a song was on the radio. Dannelle could hear a song one time and begin to sing it. They rode in the car often to the store with their dad and he listened to 92Q, an R&B station. David had driven my car and the radio was on 92Q. The song playing was "Sex how does it make you feel? Tell me if you like it, tell me it is real." My precious Dannelle was singing every word. It was at that moment when the spirit spoke and said, "If you do your part I will do mine." Immediately I turned to the gospel music station and kept it there all the time. I bought Christian videocassettes and books for my children because God was revealing to me the evil things that I, as a parent, was exposing them to. This required sacrifice on my part because I had to change, too. I thought I was a good parent, but I realized I could also be better.

David continued his busy concerts, church rehearsals, and out-of-town trips while I continued to raise these precious gifts from God. Each day before I would pick them up I would ask God, "Please tell me what you want me to teach them today." Between swim class, piano, violin, Tae Kwan Do, and church activities we were in the car a lot. We began to listen to "Focus on the Family." "Focus on the Family" offered a wealth of family-centered programs and gave you so many ideas. We listened daily while riding in the car and at home while preparing dinner. Dr. James Dobson, Christian psychologist, made things clear and simple. He promoted family and told you how to function as a family. Biblically based, it was crystal clear to me that I needed to teach my own children. Of course there were days when the broadcast would take off on political issues but we would listen to children's tapes on those days and discuss other issues. The children were really learning, and so was I. When I picked them up they would ask about the program or even when we got home they would ask. We would tune to the local Christian station, 89.1FM, even at home. I always worked with the children at home.

We watched very little TV because I was too busy teaching them how to do chores or we were practicing for something or doing homework. I always took my parenting seriously but after hearing Dr. Dobson day after day it became clearer to me the importance of being a teaching parent. I used every moment as a teaching moment and I couldn't forget hearing in my spirit, "If you do your part I'll do mine." I was determined to do my part, and I was doing it and more.

Most evenings David would come by to eat dinner and go back out whether to a meeting, concert, party, etc. We would all be asleep once he returned. One night upon his return he found me asleep in bed with my clothes on. He woke me up to tell me to put my pajamas on. Once awake I told him that if he ever came home and I was asleep in my clothes not to wake me up because I must have had a long evening being by myself with the kids. Sometimes by the time we did bath and bedtime stories, I would be wiped out. I enjoyed those evenings even though I was alone most of them. The children would often ask throughout the evening, "Where is my daddy?" And I would say, "He is working." I would never tell them he would be right back because then they would look for him. They would even ask if they could stay up until he came home and I would say, "No, you'll see him first thing in the morning." I always knew he would be there in the morning. David would get the children up for school and they would stop at the park to feed the ducks on the way to school. Evening time was sure time with Mom. There were times when I would call and ask David to pick up the children and he would really get an attitude. He never wanted to help in the afternoons with the children. After getting such a negative response from him, it would almost have to be an emergency before I asked him to pick up his own children in the afternoon.

In October 1986 we were blessed to move from Buchanan Street to Timothy Drive, a brand-new home. I was so excited to be moving from the small house that I had cried in so many days because it was so small. Valeria and Stacey, one of Mattie Kline's children, came to help me move. David had a meeting in Knoxville and wouldn't be home for the move. Mrs. Brownlee was an older friend that I could talk to. She helped to set the china in the cabinet in order. Stacey put all the things in the kitchen cabinets, and Valeria hung up clothes in the closets. The movers placed the furniture where I asked them to. When David returned home all that was left for him to do was to put the artwork on the walls. He managed to miss the entire move. The children were excited to have their own rooms. Dannelle was two years old and she would stay in her room, but most nights she would slip out of bed and come and get into our bed. She would wiggle down between us and get still. Once still, I would pick her up and take her back to her bed. She would never wake up. One day while driving home Dannelle asked, "When are we going home, Mommy?" I told her she was going home. She missed the little house. It was hard to believe she remembered it, but she did. David Jon never asked about going back. The park across the street from our new home and the playground equipment were welcomed. We would go to the park often with the children. I never sent them to the park alone. They came up during the time of the book *Never Talk to Strangers*, and many parents were beginning to pay closer attention to their children and not leave them alone.

Life remained full and busy. The children's birthdays were held together at Centennial Park. We invited the entire families to their birthday party because most had siblings around the same age. David was turning five years old, and Dannelle was turning two years old. Mom and Dad came, and Daddy brought his famous bar-b-que. All the dads at the birthday party kept trying to talk him out of his recipe. I provided corn on the cob, coleslaw, baked beans, hot dogs, drinks, and more. Their cake was a full sheet with "Happy Birthday, David Jon" on one side and "Happy Birthday, Dannelle" on the other side. We always made big birthday plans because they were born three years and seven days apart. As kids and parents began to play games, David entertained my dad and all the other dads. Of course the moms watched the children as they played games. At gift-opening time it was like Christmas. My mom even suggested we put up some of the toys for Christmas. I just listened and let the kids play with their birthday toys because Christmas would bring more toys anyway. After the families left as we packed up to leave the park we fixed plates for at least fifteen homeless people in the park. To me that was the best part of the celebration, and we still carried more food home. Once at home David Jon and Dannelle continued to play with their toys and when it came to bedtime they were so tired that after baths they went fast asleep. David and I continued to talk with my parents, who were visiting for the weekend. They soon retired also. After going over the funniest events of the day, we retired to our bedroom. After a little smooching all was quiet in the home.

David Jon and Dannelle spent that summer participating in the summer reading program. It was very rewarding because they would go to the library weekly. The summer was busy. My mom's family reunion was held in Little Rock, Arkansas, and all the Davis Family was together again. It was fun to see aunts, uncles, cousins, and other extended family. As a family trip we traveled to Florida where we went to the Kennedy Space Center, Epcot, and Disney World Theme Park. It's hard to put in writing how excited the children were. After family vacation and winding down, some of David's old high school classmates called him and said they were in town and wanted to spend the day. He was so excited on the phone, giving them directions to our home. As they came in, they were surprised to see how our home looked. I cooked a large dinner as I had been trained; I set the table etiquette style. Many memories were discussed. I sat and listened and helped the children and just observed his friends and their comments. As they were about to leave they exchanged addresses and said they would like to visit again. While rinsing and putting the dinner dishes away I could tell David was so proud of his success and how things went.

The fall of 1987 was really special. David Jon entered kindergarten. He was such an awesome handful that he had two kindergarten teachers, Mrs. Wong and Mrs. Cleaver. Mrs. Wong was a small Asian, and this was her first year teaching. On the first day she welcomed David Jon to her class and then said, "He's going to make a good football player." Immediately I knew this lady had stereotyped my child and it was going to be a long year. David Jon's class consisted of nineteen boys and five girls. The boys wrestled all the time. Mrs. Wong had little control over her class. I remembered on the first day of school we had also stopped in Mrs. Cleaver's room. Since she knew we knew Mrs. Cleaver, Mrs. Wong would take David Jon to be disciplined by her. When picking David Jon up one day Mrs. Cleaver told me David Jon was physically in her room but remained on roll in Mrs. Wong's room. Cleaver, as we fondly called her, just took my child from the little Asian. Cleaver would say, "She doesn't know how to teach our children." Whenever

D. Felecia Walker

we asked David Jon about Mrs. Cleaver he would say, "Mrs. Cleaver says she doesn't play and get my work done." Cleaver knew David Jon was a gifted child, and she kept him busy and involved all the time. She was wonderful. After graduating from Eakin Kindergarten he took the Stanford Binet achievement test and yielded a score of 99.9. This qualified him for any gifted program offered by the school district.

Dannelle was doing well at Tennessee State Early Learning Center. On her evaluation she was cited for being afraid of large costume characters. It took years for her to change her fear.

Everyone was always busy with activities. David's schedule always took us to special events like the Kappa Ball. I wore a beautiful white dress trimmed in silver that was floor length. David was always in tuxedo for most events we attended. The evening was lovely. We danced the whole evening away. I had just lost about fifteen pounds, and I was feeling wonderful, special, and real sexy. After we returned home and found the children asleep, David couldn't wait to unzip the dress and happily watch it as it fell to the floor. I knew I must have been looking really inviting because he could hardly get his clothes off. It would be nothing but love, hot love, until we fell asleep under the sheets in each other's arms. David always cuddled and lived to be right under you at night. This was every night. This was truly one part of marriage I had to get used to fast. After sleeping alone for twenty years and all of a sudden you have a "cuddler" sleeping next to you; it's a major adjustment.

Our travel schedule for the year was quite busy, too. We attended the Tennessee Black Caucus in Gatlinburg that November and just the summer before we were vacationing at Fairfield Glade and Fall Creek Falls. The children's big birthday party was held at Pizza Hut in Memphis, Tennessee, with about thirty people in attendance and all cousins and their children. My mother-in-law had purchased separate cakes for each of the children. She always did big things for her grandchildren.

Remembering Christmas that year was special because my

123

brother Matthew and his wife Jennifer spent Christmas with us. Our good friends, the Trouts, dropped by also for a visit. We always entertained, and someone was by our home quite often. David loved the holiday season and loved to put up the Christmas tree while singing Christmas carols. He would go from Handel's *Messiah* to *Christmas Blues* with music while decorating. What happy times the holidays were. I always liked the children getting so excited. Always the night before Christmas we would have to tire them out so they would go to bed early. We would bake cookies and make candy and read stories until they would fall asleep. It was always fun putting out the toys Santa Claus brought. Once we put Santa Claus's toys under the tree we knew we could go to sleep. It never failed that between 4:30 A.M. and 5:00 A.M. they were out of their beds and ready to go downstairs to see what Santa Claus left. Christmas was all so special.

In January 1988, at the first snow fall, we built two snowmen and threw snowballs. Being careful not to stay outside too long, it was back and forth to the window watching the snowfall. Inside activities were never lacking due to always having things planned to do. We were either cooking, cleaning together, watching cartoons, reading books, working puzzles, or listening to story books on tapes or making science experiments with things found in our home.

February 14, 1988:
The Valentine's Day, the Heartache, the Pain, and the Struggle

Valentine's Day was going like most all Valentine's Days with flowers sent to the job, a beautiful card on my pillow, phone calls of "I love you" while on the job, and dinner together out after work. After putting the children to bed I entered my bedroom. I went in my dresser drawer and took out my black nightie. David was already lying in bed. As I returned to the bedside David was face down in his pillow. I touched him so he could look up to see my black nightie that I knew he liked to take off piece by piece. When his face emerged from the pillow I noticed he was crying. Putting the thought of the nightie on hold, I began asking him, "David, honey, what's wrong? What's the matter? Is something hurting you?" He continued to cry. I crawled in bed and held him with his head cradled in between my breasts. I just held him as he cried; all I could do was hold him. He was unable to talk because he was sobbing so heavily. I stopped asking him and I just got quiet thinking what it could be. Once he was able to talk he said, "Deborah, I don't want to die," and I said, "What? David what are you talking about?" He repeated himself, "I don't want to die." The tears had stopped, and he said he had done a lot of things in his lifetime and had done things that were not good. He stared at the wall and then turned to me and said, "Deborah I am GAY or what they call BISEXUAL." At that moment I was in complete silence, I really couldn't digest what he had just spoken to me. I had no clue or clear understanding of what all this meant. All I knew it was Valentine's night and my hot love mood had been switched to what? Seconds and minutes make a difference.

After sitting on the bed for a moment I got up, stood to the floor trying to understand what this meant, getting up and walking the floor of the bedroom. David began to say, "Please don't leave me, please don't take my kids, please." Listening to him plead so, there was nothing I could say. I was in mental and physical shock and in desperate need of more information. You see I never really knew much about GAY people and what or how they operated. All I knew, I was married and that you can't be married and GAY because that involved same sex. The BISEXUAL was confounding me. I paced the floor until I sat on the bed. David was just quietly watching. After hours of silence I said to David, "I don't know or understand what all this means but I do know we have all sinned and come short of the glory of God. God loves you. If I claim to be a practicing Christian I must love you in spite of your confession." I can't tell you even today how I got those words out but I knew I would have to read and study for clear understanding.

That night I only slept a few hours. Upon wakening we dressed in quiet as if someone had died. I couldn't even tell you what small gift I received from him that night for Valentine's Day. I just couldn't think. Even now just to write it down, it's so painful. It's worse than opening Pandora's Box: it's painful. After arriving at work on February 15 my phone began to ring. David was calling to see how I was doing. I would quietly say, "I am doing fine or just trying to make it through today." He called and asked if we could meet for lunch and I said, "I'll just see you at home. I don't feel much like eating right now." He said "okay" and hung up. I remember that day just sitting in my office staring, only leaving out if I had to. I didn't want to see anybody really or talk; I just sat. One of my co-workers did ask me if I was okay. I worked up a smile and said, "Yeah, but you know how you have those days." I wanted to cry so badly but I was trying to work and after work I had to smile for my children and I didn't want them to be upset because if I cried they would cry. Even now I am fighting the tears and emotion.

During my work day I managed to get a dictionary and looked up the word GAY and BISEXUAL. I knew GAY was same sex but to my surprise BISEXUAL was having sex with women and men. I was ready to throw up after reading the meaning. Over and over in my mind BISEXUAL, women and men questions, over and over, how could this be? How could you be married and love me *and* men?

By the afternoon calls, I wouldn't accept them. I just needed time to think before going home. Whenever I couldn't verbally tell David my feelings I would write them down. I spent the last hour of my work day writing David a letter. David always got off work at 4:30 P.M. but he would never come home on time. On this day he was in the house at 4:45 P.M. He followed me all around the house; we ate dinner, he played with the kids and helped with baths and bedtime stories. Once the children were in bed, I gave the letter I had written to him. He sat quietly and read while I got ready for bed.

I don't remember all I wrote in the letter but I did tell him that I understood the meaning of BISEXUAL and that I didn't understand how he could be and be married. I told him he was forgiven and I just needed time to think. I could not understand how, where, when, and how it could be since we were so deeply in love and practiced intimate, hot love quite often. "Wasn't I enough?" I questioned myself and asked him the same question. He answered, "It has nothing to do with enough, and I just felt I could have it all." Struggling to understand "having it all" was even more confusing; besides, my day had been long so I quietly got into bed. He came to bed and held onto me all night. I struggled sleeping and I even got up several times through the night to cry in silence and loneliness. Whom could I tell? Who would understand? Who would laugh at me for me marrying a GAY/BISEXUAL? Didn't or couldn't I see GAY before we married? My mind was clearly tormenting me. I just cried off and on all night.

By morning my eyes were so puffy but I got up and dressed anyway and left for work. My co-workers could tell I had been crying and when they asked what was wrong I told them my sinus allergies were bothering me. Again David called all day to just say he loved me and that he was sorry. It was quite obvious that he was afraid of what was going on in my mind. After weeks of struggle he told me if I tried to leave him he would kill me and the kids. I felt the threat was certainly a lower blow because I had not given him any indication that I would ever consider leaving him. He did not need to say this to me. As I struggled I was trying to truly define who I was in our relationship and how we could move on from this point. I spent lots of time reading and thinking. Each day I kept my normal work schedule, kept the children's activity schedule, and kept everything going as usual at home.

Keeping the normalcy that I knew was real and truly hard work, but it kept me going and focused. David continued to come home every day on time as a show that he was trying to put on. Torn between sex and no sex, we began using condoms. To go from skin to condoms each time reminded me of his confession. I felt like I was being punished because the condom was coming between us. I had mixed emotions in my heart because I understood what he told me but I could hardly believe it. I guess that's why I didn't cut off from him sexually.

I asked him if we needed to go to counseling, and he said no because he was going to stay close to me. As time passed he began to tell me a few places and times where these acts would occur. It was as though I was his personal psychiatrist. He would sit and talk about his family, his childhood, and many experiences. I would listen because I realized he didn't have anyone else to talk to or listen. One night he told me that Mr. Fred was a trusted friend of his mother and that she would send him to Mr. Fred's home. Mr. Fred molested him over and over again and promised him many things if he didn't tell. Then as he got older, other boys began to experiment, and dating girls came into the experience. He never thought about the seriousness of the acts; he just focused on the feeling, fun, and how many. Just as quickly as he would bring up a conversation, he would drop it. I always listened attentively trying to put all the pieces of the puzzle together.

The Unsure Years

One evening after we put the children to bed, he was all over me with passion. I participated, but afterwards, I began to cry. He asked what was wrong, and I said nothing. He told me as I cried softly that he had never slept with a woman while we had been married. This comment just came up and out. I didn't understand him telling me this at this moment. Here was another instance of me being his personal psychiatrist. I remember saying to myself, "Is this suppose to make me happy that you haven't slept with women?" But I wondered how many men I had slept with through him. I wanted an answer to that question. This was a daily tormenting question. Each day I woke, my mind was all mixed up. I went to work and it helped me to focus on something else. I worked with my children and I kept a busy schedule. Every night I prayed that David would not have AIDS and I prayed, "Please develop medicines that would help those who were dying." I prayed without ceasing and read my Bible daily. I've had to walk with God because it would have been an even greater struggle walking alone.

As spring came in and as I continued to struggle for three months, one of my friends, Bessie Wright, asked me if I would attend a Christian ladies retreat with her. She was so up-beat about it and felt I needed something different right during this time. I agreed to go to the retreat. The retreat was over a Friday evening, Saturday, and Sunday. I left the children with their dad.

The drive to East Tennessee was simply wonderful. Just the drive and conversation took my mind off my life for moments at a time. As we arrived and saw other women, I would wonder in my mind if they came to this retreat as heavily burdened as I was. I couldn't ask anyone because I didn't want anyone to know my struggle. The activities were planned for the whole weekend with speaker sessions and classes. Private counseling was held with the main speaker. Once I heard the speaker I felt I could confide in her, so I signed up for a counseling session.

That afternoon I approached the cabin and knocked on the door. Mrs. Janie Lang met me with a smile. She was a woman of medium build who had eleven children, a minister husband, and the light flowing from her body. You could feel this person was one you can talk to. I told her my name, and I began to cry. She said, "Just take your time." When I composed myself I told her my husband told me he was GAY/BISEXUAL. She was very quiet and when she spoke she said, "Do not tell anyone." She told me that he was my husband and if he was trying to change, hang in there with him. She asked me how I was doing, and I told her my mind was tormenting me on whether to stay or to leave. She explained to me that many men have been caught up going both ways and that they are seeking ways to come out. She encouraged me to be strong in the Lord and take care of the family, carefully explaining God's plan for the family. I told her my faith in God had always been strong and I felt I could go on. She promised to pray for me and call me. We exchanged phone numbers and afterwards she prayed for me and my family.

As I returned home from the retreat, David could tell I had been renewed. By May we attended the retreat for married couples, and it helped us quite a bit. Communication was quite strong and the attention to each other was even stronger after attending this retreat. Our schedules remained busy but we were always in touch. I continued to read and we never talked about the "what ifs." We operated every day as if my much prayed prayers were being answered.

During the fall, David would often have a recital. Almost always his sinuses would get infected. He would visit Dr. Peter Jones and he would give him a prescription for antibiotics and something for a sore throat. I thought for a long time that it was a mind thing because I had heard about so many performers having problems with their vocals right before a concert. After the concert David just lay around for several days. He would go to work but he would come home, eat, and go to sleep. By the weekend he was urinating frequently and I knew something was wrong. He refused to go to the doctor as he hated to go. Besides, his doctor was dying of AIDS, and there was no one to call. After lying around most of the weekend, by Sunday morning I decided to take him to the emergency room. He began to cry and say he didn't want to go. I told him get dressed and in the meantime took the children to Sunday School.

When I returned home he was stretched across the bed. I was afraid to touch him fearing he would not wake up. I woke him up and he was putting his clothes on in slow motion. I was calling all the doctors I knew and no one was available. He was putting his clothes on and begging me to take him to church. David was minister of music at Pleasant Green Baptist Church and did not want to miss the worship service. In addition, the pianist and organist were on vacation this particular Sunday and he would have to play the piano and direct the choir. I sat nearby because I knew he was ill. I watched as he played the piano like someone under the influence. After the song before the sermon, he got up from the piano holding onto it until he reached the chair in the corner. When he got comfortable he went fast asleep. When the sermon was near ending I got up and went over to wake him up. He staggered to the piano and began playing before the sermon ended. Once the service was ended, I asked two church deacons to help me get him to the car because he was sick and I needed to get him to the hospital. He began to cry, begging me not to take him to the hospital. I told him that if he would stop crying I would take him to the walk-in clinic.

We drove to the Centra Care Clinic closest to the church. Once we arrived they put us in a room after filling out tons of registration papers and having insurance cards copied. There was a TV in the exam room so the children watched as we waited for the nurse to come in and take vital signs. When the nurse entered the room she spoke and smiled at all of us. I began to explain the events of the past week. She immediately knew something was truly wrong. She left the room and came back to draw blood for a blood sugar check. After checking his blood sugar it was over four hundred. She told me he had to go to the hospital, and he began to cry and so did the children. Seeing them all crying, the nurse left the room. I knew she was trying to get herself together because they were already crying. I stepped out into the hallway and told her I had a very emotional family. I could tell they had upset her. She told me that I needed to get him to Baptist Hospital Emergency and asked what doctor we should want her to call. I told her to call the best internal medicine physician Nashville had to offer because I had been calling doctors and couldn't get anyone. She gave me the name of Dr. Andrew Reddick. As I went back into the exam room, they were all huddled together still sobbing. I told them that we were going to Baptist Hospital, and they started crying louder. They were still crying as we left the clinic.

Arriving at the hospital I checked David in. While we waited I called Cynthia Brown and she came over to the hospital and picked up David Jon and Dannelle. Right after they left, they put David in a bed in the emergency room. We waited, we waited, we waited, we waited, we waited, and we waited. All of a sudden the curtain is pulled back and this man looking like Dr. Einstein came in. He moved slowly to tell us that he is Dr. Andrew Reddick. I thought, "This couldn't be." He looked, he poked, he felt, and basically, with zero personality, said, "I am going to order some blood tests." After the results of the blood test, David was admitted for elevated blood sugar (diabetes). He was in the hospital for seven days. Each day as I talked to the doctor, I thought he had zero personality but he knew what to prescribe. I soon realized that some brainy people had zero personality.

The call to David's parents was always a dreaded one because his mother was overly emotional. Anytime he was in the hospital she would come and stay. She would catch the first bus to Nashville. Once here she would just sit and worry. She would hardly eat, and it would be hard to get her to come home from the hospital. David had so many visitors that he caught a cold in the hospital that had to be treated because it was affecting his blood sugar level also. My mother-in-law sat with him while I worked during the day and took the children to school and I stayed with him all night. I would go to the hospital after picking the children up from school, visit a while with the children, and then take my mother-in-law and the children home. I would feed them, get them ready for bed, and then leave out for the hospital for the night. Dr. Reddick came in and said, by the fifth night, his blood sugar levels were looking better. David began to look better and feel better. My mother-in-law stayed until he came home from the hospital and then she left.

David had frequent visits to Dr. Reddick to check his blood sugar levels. He placed him on a diabetic pill to control his blood sugar. By September he was experiencing sinusitis again and was singing for the National Baptist Convention in New Orleans, Louisiana. Dr. Reddick, just as Dr. Jones, had prescribed an antibiotic for him. He was sick when he left Nashville but he didn't know how sick.

He came home back from New Orleans early and tried to work at his office. His secretary called me and asked me to pick him up from his office. I left my office and when I got there Dr. Jim Ryan was walking him to the car. I took David home. He kept saying that his head was hurting. On the back of his head near his neck were fine bumps close together and filled with pus. I gave him Tylenol and put him to bed. I called Dr. Reddick's office and they told us to come in first thing in the morning. In the meantime, I called my friend and pastor's wife who was a licensed trained nurse, Francis Barnes. I asked Francis if she would come by and take David's blood pressure. When she arrived and took his blood pressure she said it was elevated but not a lot. I told David to turn over so she could look at his head and she said he had shingles. She said, "It's a strange place to get them, but I bet you it's shingles." The next morning we went to Dr. Reddick's office. I told him the events of the evening. He sent us to the lab and when the results came back it was just as Francis said—shingles. He called a dermatologist and we went immediately to his office. He prescribed Zorivax for him and rest. Shingles are adult chicken-pox. The pox began coming out all over his body. I would bathe him three times a day and put caladryl lotion on him to dry the pox. I would wash his head also. He carried the shingles on the lower left side of the back of the head. As I bathed him day after day and week after week, I began to ponder if his immune system was starting to weaken. Our sexual contact was beginning to be less and less as he was not very strong much anymore. As he recovered and the shingles lifted and removed, it left a light pink section of the lower left side of his head without hair coming back into place. If he didn't cut his hair too low you hardly noticed it. Once we called my mother-in-law with a diagnosis she came and brought six bottles of rubbing alcohol and told me to rub his head with it. I thanked her for it and thought to myself, "If I put this on his head it would set his head on fire."

Getting ready for Thanksgiving, all was well. We traveled to Memphis for two days and returned home. My mother-in-law always cooked a lot of food and lots of family members would come by to eat. She would send us home with turkey, dressing, greens, rolls, cake, and fruits. I was always concerned about David's blood sugar because he would eat everything at holiday meals.

The Diagnosis:
Through Many Dangers, Toils, and Snares I Have Already Come

We never talked much about the possibility of AIDS, but I knew he was taking too many antibiotics too close together and he was never getting over a cold or sinusitis. Nearing Christmas 1994, David began to complain about side and back pain. I couldn't begin to figure out what this was. After hurting a couple days, I took David to the Centennial Medical Center emergency room and he was admitted for undetermined cause of pain. As the escort was pushing him through the hallway he said, "I do not want them to test me for AIDS; I do not want to know. I am not here for that." He whispered that to me in a not-so-nice tone of voice. I heard his request and I began to pray. When I called his mother she was unable to come this visit due to her having the flu. I called each night, and she was calling daily to follow his progress.

Each day Dr. Reddick would come and look at the results of test he had taken on David that day. He had tested him for everything but HIV. One evening he talked with him and told him he was going to test him for HIV because he was not responding to any of the medication. It was determined that he had a cyst on his kidney and it was removed by laser. A few days after the laser procedure the HIV blood test result came back. Dr. Reddick, who had zero personality, seemed even more withdrawn from us. On a Sunday afternoon he came into the hospital room after days of acting strangely and said, "Mrs. Walker, I need to talk with your husband alone." I felt the news wasn't good. After waiting in the hallway for several minutes Dr. Reddick asked me to return to the room. He said, "Mrs. Walker, your husband has something to tell you." I looked at

David and with fear in his eyes he said, "I am HIV-positive." I could only stand there. Once his words soaked in, I embraced him and said, "We will make it through this." I turned to the doctor and I could tell it was just as painful for him. He said, "I will come by tomorrow; just try to have a good evening." I spent the rest of the evening holding David in my arms and telling him it was okay. This was the death sentence he had run from for so long, thinking, wishing, and hoping his sexual behavior didn't catch up with him. My mind went back to when he told me he was GAY/BISEXUAL and said he didn't want to die.

As the hospital visit continued, the antibiotics prescribed by Dr. Reddick got him up and on his feet again. He told us at discharge that we need to be thinking about long-term oral medication treatment and that there were many promising drugs on the market. In the days ahead, we carried out our activities as if nothing had changed. All I knew was that we had struggled to keep things together in our relationship for five years, and I made up my mind that I had made a covenant before God and company and my husband needn't worry whether I would be there for him. I didn't know where we were going; I just knew where we had come from and what we had been through.

It had been very difficult for me emotionally not having many friends to tell my feelings to. I spent many days listening to gospel music, praying, and just meditating through the hard days. It was so hard to keep focused when so many thoughts were passing through. I knew I would have to be tested. I had been tested before, and the results were negative. I knew Dr. Reddick would want to test me again. What a heavy burden.

David began to ask Dr. Reddick to discharge him from the hospital because it was very close to Christmas. He was trying to get out so that he could purchase my Christmas presents. Once at home things were as usual. David was still quite weak. The season was festive. David Jon and Dannelle were always allowed to choose two things that they really, really wanted for Christmas. I was so happy for them, but saddened by not knowing what was going to happen next. On Christmas even our friend Leslie Shane came by to visit. She videotaped the family. She asked questions about how we planned to go into the New Year and what we wished for. We both said looking forward to family being together and health and strength. Because David was just out of the hospital, we didn't travel to Memphis right after Christmas like we usually did. We hung around home, played games, attended movies, and ate a lot. After the holidays, we were all back at our regular routines with school, work, church.

In the spring of 1995, I continued to work and take the children to various activities. One evening in April while we were eating dinner, David began to belch. He would belch for a long period of time. I called Dr. Reddick and he said he wanted to see him right away. When we visited the doctor, he scheduled an EDG test. This test allows you to look down into the stomach with a light. The morning of the test, I came into work and then I returned home so I could pick him up. In the car David was nervous. He never liked tests where they had to put him to sleep. Getting him checked in and waiting for his name to be called, we sat quietly. When we were called back, I went and sat with him. When the nurse called us back she said I couldn't go in the room. Dr. McGhee said I could come in. As David drifted off to sleep Dr. McGhee was ready to drop the light in his stomach. Once the light was inside, Dr. McGhee pointed out all the white splotches on the lining of the stomach. This was possible stomach cancer. All throughout his upper and lower stomach, there were more white splotches. I was amazed how it looked. Dr. McGhee took pictures and gave them to us for our personal viewing. The other set of pictures was for the internal medicine physician. The camera showed several ulcers also. When the test was completed David was placed in a holding area for him to wake up. When he woke up I showed him the pictures. Once dressed, we returned to Dr. Reddick's office and he viewed the pictures. He told us he would call us after talking to Dr. McGhee. Later that day it was confirmed that it was stomach cancer. At that moment David was referred to Dr. Joseph Hackworth.

Dr. Hackworth was a tall, thick man, with not much personality. He told us we could begin with three chemotherapy treatments in April, May, and July. After several questions were asked, we asked if he could take chemotherapy that would not cause hair loss. He did. During the whole course of chemotherapy, David never lost his hair. Dr. Hackworth explained that the side effects could be vomiting, nausea, weakness, stomach pain, and insomnia. After talking with him, he scheduled this first chemotherapy visit for May. When we went in for chemotherapy the nurse explained that an IV would be placed in the arm and the chemo administered through it. It took about one hour for the chemo to empty into the system. When chemo stopped, the nurse gave us discharge instructions. We left with injection needles for nausea and vitamins.

The last week of May 1996 was the annual Nashville Fine Arts Club tour. This year we were scheduled to travel to Montgomery, Alabama. We had already made reservations, and our children and two of their friends were traveling with us on the tour. We had been out of chemotherapy for about two weeks, and David still wanted to go on the trip. I could tell he was weak but since he would be riding mostly, he felt he would be all right for traveling. I stayed close by as usual. We had a good trip down to Montgomery. The tour kept us busy. Difficulties began each time we would eat. David could not hold any food on his stomach. He would vomit each time he tried to eat. He took the injection needles for nausea but they were not giving immediate relief. As our weekend progressed he became very weak. By Sunday, nearing the end of the trip, we had arrived at the historic Dexter Avenue Baptist Church for morning worship. Nearing the end of the worship, David vomited in the bathroom.

Getting him back on the bus, we headed to Nashville. At a rest stop I phoned ahead for pre-admission status and told Dr.

Reddick that David was in pretty bad shape. Upon our arrival the friends of our children got back with their parents. Dannelle went home with one of her friends and spent the night. David Jon drove us to the hospital. When we arrived at the emergency room David was taken back immediately. After I finished getting him admitted they called me back. Dr. Aimes, a physician on call for Dr. Reddick, said, "Your husband has had a heart attack. Do you have a power of attorney? Do you have a living will?" I just put my hand up as if to give him a hand in his face. He stopped asking questions. Things were moving too fast, and the doctor was making it no slower. I walked over to David and shook his shoulder and said, "David, they said you've had a heart attack." He stretched his eyes wide open and said, "What?" I repeated the words *heart attack*.

I told Dr. Aimes my husband was HIV-positive and he began to yell at me saying I should have told them when we first came in. He said they had been handling blood without using gloves. I just looked at him. By now I was in shock. A doctor yelling at me after he tells me my husband has had a heart attack. Once things settled, I got David Jon from the waiting area and we took David up to the coronary care unit. The doctor caring for him on the unit advised me to phone in his relatives. It looked pretty bad. They continued to work on him in the coronary care unit while I called Susie in Memphis to tell her David had had a heart attack. I called my parents, Miss Margie, our children's sitter, and Isaac Barnes, our pastor.

Once they had David stable, David Jon and I went back into see him. He was resting but just seeing him sent David Jon into tears. I had never seen him cry so much. I had also called Derrick and Candice Trout, who came to the hospital. Derrick took David Jon to the side and talked to him. He soon settled down. When they were ready to leave they asked him if he wanted to go home with them and he said, "No, I want to be here with my mom." Miss Margie came and sat for a while, and then the pastor came. All were very concerned about the whole family. I was crying on the inside, but I showed no emotion on the outside. When I saw David Jon crying earlier that made me want to cry. I couldn't identify with him because my father had never been ill or in the hospital for me to experience what he was experiencing. All I could do was be there for him.

Lavonia and her husband came from Memphis and brought Susie. She was worried almost to death. She went in to see David and when she came out she just cried and hollered. I could only tell her that it would be all right. I told God, "You know I have these children. Please keep their daddy for them." This was my prayer all throughout the hospital visit.

That summer was long because not only were we dealing with a heart attack, but the stomach cancer was still lying underneath. When we were able to come home, Susie was crying and walking the floor. She told David to stop smoking because that's what had given him the heart attack. He just looked at her and said, "No, Mama."

David got to work very little all that summer. He spent so much time in and out of the emergency room and vomiting.

Time approached for the second chemotherapy treatment. We feared this one because we had gone through so much on the last one. Sure enough, after about a week, David was back in the hospital. He was vomiting, had blood clots, and was just weak. Susie came again. The doctors and nurses never told her what was wrong. She always thought it was his diabetes.

When David was discharged from the hospital he told Susie it was stomach cancer. She hollered and cried and told us she was hurt because we didn't tell her. David tried to tell her that it was always so much drama behind him telling her anything that he chose not to. She said her feelings were just hurt. I stepped in and told her she made me feel as though I was not taking good care of David. I told her I was David's health care advocate, communicating with doctors, pharmacists, and nurses to assure he got the best care possible. He always had the best doctors. Our children then told her that she was always saying they were different and that it hurt when she would say David is all she had. They told her that statement hurt because it's as if she didn't accept them. She gave them a lot of material things, but the love in her heart was for that only child, David Le'ron. We all cried that day and settled some long-time hurt.

Susie soon left and the atmosphere relaxed. It was always hard when Susie visited because she stayed up all night, watched soap operas, and drank regular Coke as a diabetic. She never found out during this visit that David was HIV-positive. David knew if his mother were told this she would worry herself into the grave. She was already worried just with his day-to-day issues that she knew about. He clearly wanted to spare her of one more issue. I agreed with him.

David never lost his hair, and the chemotherapy was a success. David only had to have two chemotherapy treatments. Dr. Hackworth thought it would take three, but when the EDG was repeated the stomach cancer was gone. David returned to work in September and became strong as time went on. After having such a long summer Dr. Reddick asked us about beginning on the oral HIV medications. David agreed, and we saw a lot of improvement—so much so that we just relaxed.

The disease raised its ugly head again between 1996 and 1997 over the Christmas and New Year holiday in the form of flu-like symptoms where David had very high fevers. I was home on Christmas vacation, and I talked Dr. Reddick into letting me administer the medicine at home and it would enable us to be home over the holidays and not in the hospital. I took frequent temperatures, blood sugar checks, and made sure he was comfortable. After forty-eight hours he had to be admitted to the emergency room. When Dr. Reddick came by, he said he would administer a powerful antibiotic via IV and send us home. He felt that would do it. We were there for six hours and then discharged.

No one ever knew about our short visits but Miss Margie because she would sit with the children and make sure their activities continued as usual. I was always making sure they never missed anything because their father was ill. I knew it was our responsibility to keep them focused and functioning normally even though everything else was tense from time to time.

Getting over the flu finally got our New Year off to a good start. In the spring of 1998, I traveled to Detroit, Michigan, to attend a ladies Christian retreat with my only friend who knew, Janie Lang. David appeared stable, and in fact, it had been so quiet I was nervous. The trip was very relaxing for me and we got to talk a lot. The workshops empowered me spiritually. I remembered the last day of the retreat I sang a song for Mrs. Lang and she didn't realize I could sing. On the way back to her home we talked at length about my marriage and family situation. She encouraged me to keep on keeping on. I told her I had made a commitment and I was holding on.

Arriving at the airport I wasn't expecting what would happen to me. Taking the luggage out of the car, I began to cry. When Mrs. Lang saw me, she began to cry too. I realized I was going back to my problems and, unexpectedly, it sent me into tears. Mrs. Lang only said, "Take care and I'll be praying for you." With tears in my eyes she got in her car and drove away. I walked and cried all the way through the airport. As I sat and waited for my plane I decided I would not take another break because it was too hard to go back. Even when my family picked me up in Nashville I was still fighting the tears back. After just a weekend, it was hard coming back to face Walter (David's cocaine-addicted bisexual lover) and the ongoing issues. Walter continued to call, and David began to be absent more and more but still asking me to hang in there with him while he worked his issues out. I knew he was sexually active and continued to use drugs. He worked hard to cover, but I had learned to observe some things over a period of time.

In June, the Nashville Fine Arts Club traveled to Cincinnati, Ohio. The children and I didn't travel with David on this trip. I had begun to have a fear of traveling with him since he had the heart attack on a previous trip. I dropped him off at the bus and told him to enjoy himself. Leslie Shane, a member, had volunteered to keep an eye on him. He called each night and I was glad to hear he was fine and keeping up with the activities. Upon his return I could breathe a sigh of relief. He had made a trip event-free. Things could turn around rather quickly, but none of us were quite ready for what happened next in just a matter of a few weeks and days.

Nobody Knows the Trouble I've Seen

In June 1998, the summer began pretty quietly; there was nothing new or unusual or out of the ordinary. The children's activities had been set, and my work was beginning to pick up for the fall planning of in-service. David Jon had turned seventeen years old and Dannelle fourteen years old. Both continued to be active teens. Mom came to Nashville June 21. She would come to stay with David Jon and Dannelle while I attended the Tennessee School Food Service Association state meeting, which was being held in Memphis from Monday through Friday. I had already called my mother-in-law to let her know that I would be in town for the meeting and that we would get together on Wednesday, my free evening. The children always liked it when Mom came and so did my husband. David continued his normal work schedule, and she helped with the kids.

I had the privilege of riding to Memphis with my director, Cheryl Akins. We talked about children, spouses, family members, the job, and more. We arrived at the Crown Plaza Hotel and registered in. Once settled in the room I called home to let everyone know we arrived safely and had an uneventful trip. After saying goodbye to my Nashville family, I called my mother-in-law. She was glad to hear from me, and I told her we could get together on Wednesday evening. We talked a little longer and I told her I looked forward to seeing her on Wednesday.

After the last meeting on Wednesday I went to my room, changed my clothes, and called my mother-in-law. Susie agreed to pick me up so I went downstairs to wait. When she arrived as I got ready to open the car door she said, "Will you please drive and I will tell you how to go?" Getting under the wheel was no problem because I had ridden with her before and she would just creep along, so I was glad to drive. After speaking and hugging I asked where to and she suggested we go to Piccadilly Restaurant to eat dinner. It sounded good to me because I could get some much-needed vegetables, since I was away from home. Once inside the restaurant, the food was extremely eye-appealing, and we proceeded down the line to select our foods. At the register we argued over who would pay for the meal, and I guess you know she won. As we found seating, we began to eat and talk. We talked about how my meeting was going and then we began to discuss family issues that were on her mind. She was quite concerned about her niece, who had just left her husband and moved in with her. However, her main concern was for my husband, her son, whom she called daily and begged to stop smoking marijuana and to stay out of the streets away from persons who have the drugs. She would plead with David often but she was really worried and wanted him to stop. She asked me if he was medically doing any better, and I told her that he was continuing under the doctor's care and according to the doctor he could try harder to control his diabetes. She said, "It's hard to control your sugar because I have it and I have tried to drink diet Cokes but I can't stand them. I just have to have a regular Coke." Feeling her concern, I assured her that God was in control and we must continue to pray for Lavonia and David, and she agreed because only the Lord could change things. As we finished our meal and prepared to leave, I could tell just our visit seem to have lightened her heart.

As always when we would talk or be together she would remind me that her full-length fur coat was mine if she ever passed away and I would say, "You're not going anywhere." As we drove back to the hotel to drop me off we mostly discussed the children and their activities and when they would be in Memphis for their summer visit. As I pulled the car over in a space in front of the hotel, preparing to say goodbye, my mother-in-law said, "Deborah, I know it's hard to help David but just keep praying." I told her it was difficult and I told her I would stay with him and continue to help him with his health, and I would do the best I could. As she drove away slowly I went to my room, giving her time to get home. I called and she had made it and I thanked her for a good evening.

When Friday came I had planned for Aunt Annie to pick me up in Memphis. Mom and the children came later because we visited with Aunt Annie two nights and went to Pine Bluff so we could drop Mom at home. Visiting Aunt Annie has always been a special treat. There are only eight thousand or so people in Batesville, Arkansas, and the biggest shopping event is at the local Wal-Mart. When Mom and the kids arrived, Mom talked about what a good job David Jon had done driving them over. Aunt Annie was so glad we were spending the night with her. She had prepared a big dinner for us. After eating we always headed out the door for Wal-Mart. Aunt Annie, in her eighties, loved to ride the electric wheeled carts because it enabled her to follow us throughout the store. She kept telling the children to get something and whatever they picked up she paid for it. Mom and Aunt Annie are big quilting buddies so we could not leave the store before looking in the fabric section. On the way back to Aunt Annie's house we stopped at Dairy Queen for ice cream. We could never pass Dairy Queen without stopping. Once inside the house that night I called David in Nashville to let him know we had arrived safely in Batesville.

I asked him to let his mother know because she would always worry whenever she knew we were traveling. The children said hello and we told David good night. After staying up late watching TV and talking, we got ready for bed. Rising early the next morning before daybreak, we headed to Pine Bluff. I could tell Mom was glad to be going home after a week away from home. Batesville was two hours from Pine Bluff, and we arrived just in time to wake Daddy up and eat breakfast. As always we called back to let Aunt Annie know we arrived safely in Pine Bluff, and as always she said we made good time. After hanging the phone up, David Jon and Dannelle woke Daddy up. He was kissing everybody and just plain glad to see us. Mom busied herself fixing breakfast and unpacking and looking over the house since she had been gone a week. While the children talked with Daddy, Mom and I got breakfast on the table. After prayer Daddy began to eat and tell the children funny family stories. Their favorite is about a preacher who came to preach at his father's church and had a wooden peg leg. The floor of the church was natural wood and had holes in it. When the Holy Ghost rested on the preacher he began to run and shout with that wooden peg leg, and it got caught in one of the holes and pulled it off. The preacher, missing his wooden peg leg, fell to the floor and continued to wiggle and preach as if nothing had happened.

After hearing the many laughs, Mom and I cleared the breakfast dishes. I always liked to poke around in Mom's room because her sewing machine and dress patterns were all around. Remember, my mom is super gifted with her hands and I always call her Dorcus. Mom has made clothes for everyone in our family at one time or another and she is still making my clothes.

The visits home never seemed long enough as our time grew closer to leaving. We left Pine Bluff early on Sunday after attending church with Mom and Dad so we could stop in Memphis to visit my mother-in-law. As we said our goodbyes I also thought about coming again.

Driving from Pine Bluff to Memphis, we listened to gospel music, and the children played video games and worked on travel puzzles. They always knew how to busy themselves on long trips.

Arriving in Memphis, Lavonia met us at Susie's door. She told us Susie had gone out with two of her other nieces. Lavonia said that Susie had been hopping on her leg and said she could hardly walk. I was sorry to hear that but I thought to myself, "It must not be too bad if she is not at home resting her leg." We told Lavonia to tell Susie we came by and we traveled on to Nashville.

Upon arriving, David told us that they had called him and

rushed his mother to the hospital. I told him she was not at home
when we stopped so I felt like it must not have been too bad
since she was not at home. As the children unpacked the car and
retired themselves for bed Lavonia called to say she was back
home from the emergency room. They had given Susie some
kind of medicine and said she would be better by morning.

It was back to work for me, and we were all in our normal
routines. David called me off and on throughout the day to let
me know Susie was still not doing too well.

On Tuesday June 30, David had an 8:30 A.M. doctor's
appointment as usual with Dr. Reddick. We arrived and once in
the exam room we told him about Susie. After checking David
out and reading his lab results Dr. Reddick told David his blood
sugar was not controlled and if any little thing happened he
would be in trouble. He increased his insulin, and our visit to
the doctor's office ended. Arriving at the office, Lavonia called
David and told him she had taken Susie to the hospital because
she was not improving. David called me at work and told me he
was going to leave and go to Memphis for as long as it took to
see about Susie. I told him to be careful and call me as soon as
he heard something.

By Wednesday or Thursday her doctor had confirmed that
she had suffered a stroke. She was able to recognize people
but she could not walk. As we decided, David came home and
picked all of us up and we headed for Memphis. It was now the
Fourth of July weekend. Susie was in a private room, and David
was spending his days and nights at the hospital. The children
and I were with Lavonia at the house and went to the hospital for
short visits. David had cried and he was beginning to look tired.
Remembering what Dr. Reddick said, I knew he needed his rest,
but I also knew he was not leaving his mother's side. With little
improvement it was getting harder to understand what was happening to Susie for David.

David was minister of music at church so he told Lavonia
we would go back home and that he would be back early

Monday morning to be with her again. We arrived in Nashville just in time for church service. David directed the choir as usual, greeted members at the end of service, and we went home.

That afternoon, finishing dinner and unpacking clothes, David called Lavonia and the hospital; still no change. Once he told me what they said, the children and I took a short nap. When I woke up David was gone to Walter's house. After spending time with him he returned home high as a kite. He was eating everything in the kitchen he could put his hands on. I knew he was high, and it didn't seem to matter to him that he was either. He was trying to cope and get lost in his mother's sudden illness.

After watching a movie that night with the family, David told me he was going back to Memphis in the morning. I told him to go to bed so he could get a good night's rest and he said, "I'm coming. I just want to watch the news." I woke up at 2:00 A.M. and went to the restroom as usual. David was in bed and snoring hard. He was tired, and I was glad he was resting in bed. Morning came as usual. I got up, dressed, and went to work as always. Miss Margie came and picked up David Jon and Dannelle and carried them to their activities as always. David remained asleep as no one talked to him before they left home trying to give him much-needed rest.

At work it was busy as usual. My co-workers were asking about my mother-in-law because they knew I had just seen her the week before in Memphis. I had not heard from David, but I thought that he probably slept late and left late before going to Memphis.

Arriving at home I prepared dinner for the children and myself. We began to talk and play around and then completed some chores around the house. Just before they went to bed Lavonia called me and told me something was wrong with David. She said he was talking slowly and she felt his blood sugar must have been really high. I told her to let me talk to him. When he got on the phone he was talking slowly and making no sense. I told him to put Lavonia on the phone. I said, "Lavonia,

I am coming to Memphis to bring him back to Nashville so his doctor could check him out." None of the relatives or his mom knew he was HIV-positive. I knew he needed to get back to his own doctors. At that moment, she said, "Deborah, someone traveled with him today." When I asked who it was, she said it was Walter. I told her to put that no-good dope-smoking dealer on the phone. I asked Walter how long he had been like that, and he said since he picked him up. He said he begged David to call me but he wouldn't. At this point, he seemed nervous. "He just kept asking for his mother so he went on and drove him to Memphis. After dropping me off at a friend's home he drove to the hospital and then drove back over to his mother's house. I walked back over here, and his cousin told me she was going to call you." I told Walter to put David in the car and bring him straight to Centennial Medical Center emergency room. I said, "Walter, do not stop anywhere; just bring David to the hospital." When he handed the phone back to Lavonia, he told her he was not going to the hospital to face me and she told him to take David straight to the hospital like I had instructed.

After they left Lavonia called me and said to me what Walter had said to her. She knew David was on drugs. I told her, "Lord have mercy on us with Susie in the hospital in Memphis and David coming to the hospital in Nashville." I questioned, "Lord, how much more?" Getting off the phone with Lavonia I called our family friends Candice and Derrick to tell them what had happened. As it would happen Derrick had seen David with Walter and talked to David and knew he looked and talked a little strange. When he saw David, he told him he was going to call me, but he never did. He apologized for forgetting. I told Candice I would be in touch soon. While going over in my mind and getting myself together I called Dr. Reddick for pre-admission status and explained to him what had happened. After talking to him I called Miss Margie over to spend the night with the children. She had spent quite a few overnights as we would call her on various hospital visits.

Miss Margie came and we fussed about Walter driving David all the way to Memphis knowing he was sick. I got up and began to get things pulled together around the house before leaving for the hospital. I talked to the children as I had always done before and explained to them that their father was sick and I didn't know what had happened to him. I told them that Miss Margie was there and she was staying the night. We hugged as always and Miss Margie said, "Baby, hold on." She always encouraged me even though she was unaware of the HIV.

Arriving at the hospital emergency room I registered David in and told the clerk and nurse he was on his way in from Memphis. They told me that Dr. Reddick had called in just as he had called in so many times before. I sat down and watched the parking lot. While keeping watch I could only think, "Where are we going now?"

I could soon see the brownish-gold car in the distance. It was around 2:00 A.M. I told the attendant with the wheelchair that they had arrived. As we stepped out of the emergency room into the driveway, the car was traveling so slowly. We soon realized that David was driving and was very much alone. Barely driving onto the parking lot, and barely missing a row of cars, I just screamed, "Stop the car! Please stop the car!" The attendant ran to the car with the wheelchair and got him out. I parked the car as they took him into the emergency room.

David was in pretty bad shape. He was unfocused and his speech unclear. He seemed to understand that he was now in the hospital. I just sat by the bed and waited for the doctor to come. Running many tests while in the emergency room took its usual time. It was 5:30 A.M. We were moved to the eighth floor because the nurses on all shifts knew our situation and had grown accustomed to our visits.

As we sat in the room I kept trying to talk to David. He would look at me and smile. The nurse came in and asked him his name, and he couldn't speak his name. As the morning progressed and more tests were run, Dr. Reddick told us that he had

had a stroke. The speech problem was due to aphasia, a neuro-logical disorder that accompanies a stroke. This hospital visit was the most challenging ever. I could not tell in what direction we were going. When the children came to visit the doctor asked, "Who is this, David?" And he said, "My children." He never called them by name; he would simply say they were his children. When asked who I was, he would just look at me and smile. He was never able to call my name. He was still able to toilet himself, but needed assistance dressing because of right-sided weakness. His right side was not responding well. When I touched his right foot there was no feeling in it on the bottom; his left foot responded because he would laugh out loud because it tickled him. Each time the children came he would say, "My children, my children," and smile.

In 1996 we had plans drawn to build a new home and had selected a lot. The project was well underway. Once David was hospitalized with the stroke I asked him whether we should continue and he said yes. He was always sleeping off and on. By this time, he was on so many medicines that the nurses were confused trying to administer them so I told Dr. Reddick we would bring medications from home. Dr. Reddick wrote this in the chart. Strangely enough, David could still give himself his insulin shots. The nurse would watch him closely, though, as I looked on.

Day after day while staying in the hospital pretty much night and day, we continued to talk to the first cousins from Memphis about Susie's progress. Each day we would call so he could talk to his mother. I would say to David say *Mama* and it would take a while to get it out. She also had difficulty speak-ing, and I wonder what she thought about what he was saying and not saying. Those moments were so hard to observe. As they would end the conversation I would talk to whoever was in the room at the time. David's cousin Jeanie kept calling me and asking me about Susie's personal business. I told her we knew nothing and when I would ask David, he would just shrug his shoulders with no response. After many phone calls about her personal business I told Jeanie that I was David's power of attorney and if a decision was to be made, I would have to make it on his behalf. I could feel myself being totally aware at this point because I knew and realized my burden had just gotten a little heavier.

Since we were in Nashville and they were in Memphis, Jeanie obtained power of attorney for her Aunt Susie. This allowed her to write checks and handle her personal business. She proceeded to remove David's name from his mom's checking and savings accounts and added her own name. She continued to call and ask several questions about her for which we had no answer. Lavonia called me and said, "I don't know what is going on. At first I was helping her and now she's not telling me much. She has just taken over." After hearing this long-distance, I knew it was nothing I could do. My hands were full because David was not improving. Jeanie talked about putting Susie in a nursing home, and I told her that would be fine because I may have to put David in a care facility because of his physical state. Nothing was clear.

In the back of my mind I knew we had been in the hospital several days. We began to get the letters from the insurance company stating they would not pay the bills because his condition was not that serious. The insurance company was also threatening not to pay the hospital bill because we were using our medicine from home and I was issuing them to him. He was taking morning medicine, lunch medicine, and supper medicine. It was about five to ten pills at a time with some being given at one time, others two times, and then all three. I would have to be so organized. I had memorized his pill boxes. He would take the insulin at each meal.

As pressure built up Dr. Reddick told us he had gone to administration and got a few more days approved. The social worker came by and the psychologist. After the psychological exam his tests revealed that he was too high-functioning for a residential situation; however, he could not be left alone because of the aphasia, which is the inability to express what you want to say. I was stressed not knowing what I would have to do. We had soon been in the hospital for three weeks. On July 24, 1998, the hospital administrator came to David's room and told us the insurance company would not pay the hospital bill so we would have to leave. I remember being so angry gathering up his things to take home. I didn't have anyone to turn to. We left the hospital for home. Once at home I called Lavonia in Memphis to tell her we were home. She asked if we were coming to Memphis, and I told her that it was just too soon to know if he could travel or not because Dr. Reddick suggested that he not travel. It would be too much stress. Susie remained in the hospital and we continued to communicate daily. She was not progressing much at all.

After the weekend and much thought, I knew I had to get someone to sit with David. I decided to ask Miss Margie. Realizing I would have to tell her about his HIV, I knew I would have to trust her with our secret. As I began to tell Miss Margie everything, she sunk back in the chair and began to cry. After telling her she said, "Baby, are you all right?" and I answered, "Yes." She hugged me and told me to hold on and that she would sit with him. The weight had lifted because finally someone knew who seemed to understand and who was encouraging me.

By the next Saturday and just having talked to Susie Friday night, Lavonia called and said, "She's gone." I just sat on the bed speechless. Once I could talk again I said, "What?" and she repeated herself. I said "What? What happened?" Lavonia stated no one was with her and the nurse said she had some problems breathing. Jeanie told them to put the breathing tube in, and she passed away. (Silence on the phone.) I asked her, "Girl, how am I going to tell David?" and she said, "I have no idea." I told her I would call her later.

Susie had passed away never knowing David was HIV-positive. We had managed, through all the hospital visits and phone calls and her visits to our home, to spare her of that piece of bad news. I couldn't help but thank God because news of that earlier would have killed her. She loved David so much but had no idea of the burden he was carrying.

Knowing he couldn't talk much and express himself, I just couldn't tell him right away. I told the children, and they both cried in their rooms so not to let on to what had happened. I couldn't cry because he would have known by my face turning red. This was so hard. I called my parents, and my mother said she would come right away from Arkansas. When I hung up the phone, Jeanie called. She said she could not believe it and said, "You know, she was scheduled to go to the nursing home on Monday." She asked me when we were coming to Memphis, and I told her I needed to talk to David's doctor first. I told her we had not told David just yet. I was still trying to get myself ready for his response, remembering how he screamed and crawled the floor when finding out his father had passed six years before. I just dreaded going through that again.

As I sat quietly I thought to call Isaac and Francis Barnes. Isaac was our minister at church. They came over around 6:30 that evening. My friend, Janice, just happened to stop by as they were coming in. I pulled her aside and told her. I explained to her that he did not know yet but we were about to tell him. As they all looked on, I said, "David, Lavonia called and said Susie passed away this afternoon." At that moment his eyes enlarged in shock of what he had just heard and he began to cry. We were all encouraging him and holding him. To my surprise he was quiet. There was not loud sobbing at all. He just sat quietly.

Isaac talked to him and by the time they left he had stopped crying. Soon after, people began to call, one right after the next. Making sure David was eating right and taking his medicines, I kept close watch on him. On Sunday the phone began to ring, and after church, people came by to visit. David remained quiet. I would sit with him, hold his hand, and tell him everything would be all right. Mom arrived and gave me tremendous support. Because David could not communicate, I was left answering all the questions. If anyone had ever told me that my husband would not be able to communicate, I would have never believed them. All I could think about was how was I going to know people's names when we got to Memphis, and how David's health would be. Lord Jesus, my mind was spinning. I knew the week would be hard. It was no time for running up and down the road because David's health could change at any time. After talking to Dr. Reddick, getting prescriptions filled, and talking to my director at work, we left for Memphis.

When we arrived, people were all over the house. Just a small five-room house, there was almost standing room only. In just the time that Mom had been with us, Mom had managed to help David say "hi" and "hello" so he could greet people as they came in. Once they recognized he could only greet them and smile, they would began to talk to me. I talked to so many people I didn't know. I had prayed, "God, please place your ministering angels all around me to protect me during this time because I knew this time would be most difficult and conflicts were sure to arise. I had asked my mom to clean up the kitchen. I knew I had to go through that house because we didn't have time to waste.

The first cousins had written the obituary. As I read through it, I began to tell them that it could not be printed yet as it was written. I could tell they were in shock at my speaking up because they always saw me as quiet and David's little wife and the mother of his children. They had written David's half-brother on the program first, putting them in the order as they were born. I told them that the obituary was a historical docu-ment and that David was the only child born to Susie Walker and the step-children, who were never adopted by her, were only step-children. I said to them it should be listed on the obituary as David L. Walker, son, Deborah, daughter-in-law, David Jon and Dannelle Walker, grandchildren, and then to list the step-children and the host of nieces, nephews, and friends. When I finished, they were quite confused.

In black families everybody raises you, and you can hardly tell who is a true relative. My immediate family was not like this, and I knew right from wrong. While I understood that everyone was raised by Susie in the family, I knew that, for historical purposes, everyone was not Susie's biological child. I did set the record straight to their being upset about it. While still working with them, Jimmy, David's step-brother, came by. He came in through the kitchen door and rudely greeted my mom, who was working to clean the kitchen. He told her to stop because Susie had just died. I didn't appreciate the way he talked to my mother. I told Mom to go to bed and when he was at home, we would begin our work again. People are always trying to stop progress and not thinking about offering to help. Sonia finished the obituary and we told her we would take it to the funeral home in the morning.

When morning came, Mom and I were up really early and finished cleaning the kitchen. We agreed that Lavonia, David's cousin who was like a sister to him, was going to live in the house. She was so glad we were cleaning everything out. I had told David before we left home that we had to do what we had to do, and he was okay with it. Before we arrived, Jeanie and others had gone through Susie's papers. No one had located an insurance policy. Jeanie had called us before we left Nashville to tell us she had not found a policy anywhere. She also explained that she and Lavonia had picked out the casket and clothes for Susie to wear. Jeanie told us that my mother-in-law had only two thousand dollars in the bank and the funeral cost five thousand. She also stated that Susie was behind in her property taxes by fifteen to seventeen hundred dollars. She said we needed to bring these monies when we came to Memphis. I took the money out of my retirement annuity because we had just paid six thousand dollars out on David's leased car. We paid six thousand cash. Earlier we borrowed from our first life insurance policies to make a down payment on our home. I was under mental stress like you wouldn't believe, and everything was on me all at the same time.

As people continued to come and go, we continued to go through paperwork between the visits. By evening, Jeanie came over. When she realized we were cleaning out closets, she said she had seen Susie in a dream and she said, "Tell those Negroes not to bother my stuff." Lavonia took her out of the house and talked to her and she finally went home. Lavonia told me Jeanie was crazy for saying that because she had not been as close a niece to Susie as she was claiming to be. Lavonia said that if Susie would appear to anyone it would be David because she loved him and she said, "I haven't seen her and I've been living with her." She told me to keep doing what I was doing.

Overhearing the conversation, cousin Martha began to help me go through the papers. As we were cleaning and going through things, everyone kept asking about the fur coat of Susie's. It was not in the house and I didn't have a clue where it was. Every time I visited Memphis, Susie would tell me that if she died, her fur coat was for me, and to get the cedar chest to the bedroom suite. I told her, "Oh, don't talk death talk; you're not going anywhere." I was wrong. As Martha continued to help, she came across a pink piece of paper. It was from King's Furs. As things go she had put the fur in for cleaning and storage on June 3, 1998. Martha gave me the ticket and told me to call them. I called the fur shop and they confirmed the coat was there. I told him Susie had passed and they told me I could pick up the coat and hat at any time. I told Martha what they said and she said, "Don't say anything about that coat to anyone; just pick it up and take it to Nashville when you leave." She remembered Susie telling her about the coat and shared with me how she felt cleaning out Susie's house was good because her mother had been dead for two years and they never got together to clean her home out. She said she realized I had a sick husband and a lot was on me and she said, "You just got to do what you've got to do."

The funeral was set for Saturday morning. We had arrived on Monday so we had plenty of time to get things in order. By Thursday, everything was organized, and I told her nieces they could have their aunt's things. I told them to take whatever they wanted. Many of them kept saying, "She's not buried yet," while others picked out what they wanted. Even worse, some wore her clothes to the funeral. David woke up early Thursday and told me his tooth was hurting, so I had to take him to the dentist. This was frightening to me because I knew HIV patients' teeth were delicate because of the medication they were taking. We got in to see a dentist and he prescribed antibiotics because David had an abscess around the tooth. I told David we would see the dentist after we returned to Nashville.

On Thursday evening, I asked Cousin Sonia to take us downtown on Friday morning. She didn't question me at all. She always liked me because she knew my heart. She and David would party together on occasion when we would travel to Memphis. She soon stopped before we had children so we didn't visit her as much, but she remembered me. Jimmy came by late that night after Lavonia had taken David to the store and was questioning me about the insurance and money. I told him we found a policy and it paid two thousand dollars because Susie had lied about her age, and that she died broke. We had no money for funeral, taxes, or bills. It all ended up on David and me.

Friday morning Sonia picked us up, and no one knew where we were going. Susie had told us David had property and we went downtown to see that in writing and pay the property taxes. We were able to pay all the taxes while there, and the properties were transferred from Susie's name to David's and the children's names. I never have wanted material possessions; I just wanted to see that my children get what is rightfully theirs and what they should have. That's why, before David ever had the stroke, we wanted to build a nice house so that if something happened to us, we would have left our children with good investment in property.

Time was nearing for the bank to close. David wanted to go to the bank because he couldn't believe his mother only had two thousand dollars in the bank. I continued to pay the taxes, and I told them I would meet them in front of the building. When we got back together Sonia was furious; she said that Jeanie had taken David's name off the accounts and he had no access to the accounts. He was clearly upset. Susie had told everyone she had plenty of money, and everyone believed her. To their surprise, but not mine, I knew she and David spent money like it grew on trees. As soon as we got back to the house Sonia explained to Lavonia what Jeanie had done. It became clear that she was being underhanded. Jeanie had told several cousins she was not going to let me take over. There was drama as I suspected.

People were still coming by and for the first time in several days I sat down and ate. I had everything in order and I knew Saturday would be hard.

The funeral. We had gone to the wake and Susie looked real good in her casket. I knew we would see so many people on Saturday. Just as most nights, we got to bed late. Waking up early, it was hard getting dressed. I just felt weighed down and I could hardly get going. David was quiet, and people were calling to express their sympathy. After getting dressed, the funeral cars picked us up and we headed for the church. Several family members, friends, and others were there to greet us. As the funeral director lined us up to go in, I knew this was it. Dr. Franklin Jones, officiating the service, had baptized David as a child and had been their minister since before David was born. As we processed into the church people were still viewing the body.

We were seated, David began to cry silently. I had put several pieces of tissues in my purse, so I gave him one right after the other until he settled down. I was so emotionally drained and felt physically whipped. During the services, everyone else's tears would fall, but I still had not cried.

After the funeral and to the cemetery while riding in the car, David's half-brother Harold looked at me and said, "He sure takes good care of you," and I said, "We've taken good care of each other."

Entering the cemetery, I couldn't believe we were about to say our final goodbyes to Susie. Susie, a mother, grandmother, a person whom I struggled to get to know better and with whom I wanted to be close. She was so different from the women I had been exposed to growing up. I could only resolve that I had done the best I could do in a relationship where the mother was so crazy about her child that she couldn't see her daughter-in-law or the grandchildren. All I could whisper over her casket was, "No more worries. You can rest now; just rest." I smiled. I put the last flowers I could give her on her casket.

After we left the cemetery, we went back to the church for dinner with friends and family. Many people we had not seen in several years were there. The fellowship was great for David even though his communication was limited. Before we left the church, we thanked the church members who had prepared a wonderful meal. As we left to return to the funeral cars, I couldn't believe they had stayed with us all day.

Dropping us off at home, people began to come by. David and I changed clothes. In the back of my mind I knew we were leaving for Nashville in the morning and I thought, "How can I pick up the fur coat without anyone knowing about it?" In came Tonya, who was the girlfriend of T.J., Lavonia's son. No one in the family really knew Tonya, so I told everyone she was taking me to the store. No one knew what store, and no one knew Tonya. We got in the car and I told her that Susie had left me the coat and it was at the fur store and I didn't know my way around in Memphis, but we had to try. We got on Poplar Street and, to my surprise, it was across the street from a mall Susie had taken us to in the past. I entered the store and gave the clerk the pink ticket. He told me it would be seventy-five dollars, and he gave me a bag to store the coat in. The fur hat was in a nice hat box. As we traveled back to the house I told Tonya to take the coat in and no one would pay any attention to her. Jeanie was on the front porch and as I walked up she said, "Did you all ever find the fur coat?" I just didn't answer. All evening people were coming and going. There was plenty of food and drinks, and funeral plants were everywhere. We told everyone we were going home Sunday afternoon, and we got into bed late again. I was so tired I felt I had no body. I thanked God for allowing us just to make it through the day.

Early Sunday morning, Jeanie called and said she was bringing all the paperwork from Susie over. We got up and dressed. I called Lavonia and told her so she came down from the upstairs apartment. When Jeanie arrived, she was still asking about the coat. She even went to the upstairs apartment looking for it. Tonya, who spent the night, heard her coming and put the coat in the bed with her. Jeanie never found the coat. As we waited for her downstairs Lavonia was saying, "She ain't right." David and I listened. Jeanie didn't know what we knew, so we just let her talk. David had put a hold on the account so she couldn't write any more checks. We thanked her for all her help, and she said she would come back after church to see us off. I told David to rest after she left. He looked so tired.

The phone rang and Janice, my friend from home, had visited her mother in Arkansas and was on her way back to Nashville. She asked if it was anything she could do and I said "yes." She came by and we put all the plants and my fur coat in her car. She ate lunch with us and left for Nashville. I could only smile inside.

While packing our car, Jeanie came back still asking for the fur coat. Lavonia and I almost burst open trying to keep from laughing. We gave Jeanie a quilt, and she got whatever else she wanted. She asked for the cedar chest, and David pointed to me. As we said our thanks and goodbyes, I told Lavonia to do whatever she needed to do to be comfortable in the home. I had made arrangements for the other two renters also. I felt good leaving Memphis that day, feeling that closure had come and things had been organized.

Listening to my gospel tapes, I thanked God I had made it through the drama-filled family members. They should never speak a bad word about me because I was and had been taking care of my and our responsibilities. They didn't have a clue that their cousin was so ill, nor did the brothers know their brother was so sick.

Back in Nashville after a long week I was so glad to be home. We unloaded the car and put things away. David took the Sunday paper and began to call words out loud. My mother told him to practice reading out loud because that would help to exercise his brain.

The next morning everyone slept late while I went back to work. It was a full day. I had missed opening school in-service so I had to sort through all the materials brought back from the meeting. David Jon and Dannelle were home with David so I knew things were okay. In the evening, David would walk up and down the street because he was so frustrated at not being able to drive. He would walk off, and people would call me saying they saw him. This got to be an every-afternoon occurrence. I finally told one neighbor, "Look, I am at home. He has ID in his pocket and I am at home; if something happens someone will call me." I just believed that.

Even though we had suffered the loss of my mother-in-law, we began to break ground on our new home that we began planning back in 1996. At the ground-breaking were several friends and our pastor and his family. Our pastor prayed over the site, and we all walked around just wondering what it would eventually look like. I can't begin to explain the joy way down inside I felt that day. God was blessing in a special way all in the midst of ongoing tragedy and suffering. We were beginning a faith walk because we had no clue about building a house and what it involved. All I knew was that we had qualified and the paper-work was complete and we were beginning the process. My daily work was too busy to let me worry about the new house. I just felt it would work itself out. This venture gave all of us something to look forward to. I wanted to see the house project through because I wanted David to know that even though he was disabled, I wanted us to still have what we had planned together as a family. I was unsure of the days ahead, about his health and our finances; but I felt I was already going through so much, so what would more going through do but produce results and more strength?

It was time for school to begin. This was David Jon's senior year. He was so excited, and I was too. In the background I was trying to figure out what I would do about David once school started. I thought to myself, I'll ask Miss Margie if she would stay with David.

Miss Margie would come each morning just before the children would leave for school and stay until I got home from work. She would take David to the doctor and I would meet them and also she would drop him off at speech therapy. I would pick him up from speech therapy and then pick up Dannelle from school. Most days I felt like I had three children. Speech therapy time had been set up so I could pick David up just after I left work. Miss Margie would drop him off, and she would be off for the day. David would go with me everywhere. He was physically getting along pretty well. Miss Margie would take him wherever he pointed out the way.

By October we had a good routine going. I attended speech therapy and occupational therapy with David. The speech thera-pist said David was pretty stubborn about doing his therapy exercises. He always wanted to do bigger things but frowned on the small steps of speech therapy. In occupational therapy they were daily working on the driving video. David was really looking forward to driving again so this therapist told him dur-ing his visits he was doing quite well. I was so uneasy about him returning to driving. He just couldn't communicate, and he was not focused mentally.

About mid-October after arriving at work and settling in for the day, David Jon called me and said David had fallen next to the bed. Miss Margie arrived, and I told her I was on my way home. I took David to the hospital. He never liked going to the hospital so I would tell him, "We're going and then I'm going to bring you on home." He would then settle down. Once checked in and as tests were run, he had another stroke. I called the Reverend Eddie Landers, one of David's long-time friends, because they were to meet for breakfast.

Just as he entered the hospital room and greeted David, David began to have a gran mal seizure. I had never experienced anything like this seizure. He drew his arms close to himself, his legs were in a fetal position, and his tongue was hanging from the mouth. I was holding on to his arms as they drew up and as his body was twisting. I was screaming as loud as I could, "Oh Jesus, oh Jesus, oh Jesus." When I looked at the nurses they were motionless, so I thought, "Why?" I shut up and they said he was having a seizure. Eddie, being a man, just stood by. I thought David was dying. If you've never seen a seizure it is a phenomenon.

After the seizure had passed he slept and wet himself. The nurse had prepared me for this. She also told me it could recur within thirty minutes. When thirty minutes passed he seized again. This time I was calm and just held on to his arms. Eddie prayed over him and left after the second seizure. Dr. Reddick came in and told me that Dr. Calvin would be in to see David. When Dr. Calvin came by he told me they would add to his medications Dilantin, which is medication for seizures. When David woke up, he did not have any knowledge about what had happened to him and when I tried to tell him, he just couldn't believe it. As the day went on there were no more seizures, so the medication was indeed working. Before this happened we had planned to fly to Chicago for David's first cousin's birthday.

I told him we could not take the trip, and he cried. He wanted to go so badly, and I wanted to take him. I just couldn't take the risk of traveling so far without his doctors. This was too much stress for me.

Every day was moving pretty routinely, and David and Miss Margie were doing fine. However, event-free days were lacking. One morning after I arrived at work, being there for about two hours, David Jon came to my office. David had gotten up early and turned the radio on loudly in our bedroom. David Jon turned the music down and David turned it back up loud. They began to fight a while and Dannelle tried to break it up. Before the fight ended David had bitten David Jon in the face. David Jon still did not know his Dad was HIV-positive, nor did Dannelle.

After arriving at the office and hearing his story, I called Dr. Reddick. He assured me that there was little virus in the saliva and he was sure that David Jon was fine. After talking to Dr. Reddick, I put an alcohol pad on David Jon's facial bite and told him to go on to school. About an hour later Miss Margie was at my office. David had asked her to bring him there to talk to me. I told Miss Margie I was on my job and that I was too upset to see him right then. She went out and told him what I said. After they returned home Miss Margie called me and said David wanted to talk to me. I told David he knew he was HIV-positive and he had no business fighting his own son. I told him, "I just don't have the strength to take care of two HIV-positive persons. It would just be too much." I began to cry so I told him bye. Miss Margie called later to make sure I was okay. And as usual she told me to just hold on. After this incident I kept as close a watch as I could on David and David Jon's contact to make sure there was no more wrestling. It was too high-risk, and I knew my hands were already full. David Jon was later tested and was free of HIV.

With the house coming up, senior year, and Thanksgiving I was too excited underneath the weight. My family came for Thanksgiving and it blessed my heart so. My mom was busy helping David with his speech, my brother and his wife were expecting twin boys, my two younger nieces kept each other company while everybody else sat around watching movies and talking. Mom and Dad had made the turkey dinner, and all I had to do was set the table. The dinner was wonderful and as usual we were all stuffed afterwards.

Friday morning after breakfast we all went on a field trip to the new home site. It was quite impressive with the framing complete, bricks laid, and windows in. Daddy was telling me things to check for, and everyone else was just walking through and asking about what each room was. After the field trip everyone was on their way home. We had our home back for the remainder of the holiday weekend.

Therapy was coming along well and David was beginning to get more and more excited about driving. David Jon was playing basketball, and we attended all his games in town and out. People seemed to adjust to David's inability to communicate, but I would talk and get us over the conversation. It was quite awkward most of the time.

Christmas that year just had a different feel. With my in-laws deceased it was just different. With the children being older and knowing there was no Santa Claus, we had to work up a joyous spirit. As our time at home together progressed, Christmas was becoming better.

January 1999 came in and this was the month David had been looking for. Tennessee law states that you must wait six months after a stroke before you can drive again and you must take a driving test. Vanderbilt Stallworth where David had been taking occupational therapy referred him to the Nashville Rehabilitation Hospital to take a driving test. Miss Margie called me and said she was taking him and I said, "Lord, have mercy." She replied, "I hear ya." After the test Miss Margie called me to say David passed the driving test. We just couldn't see how. We figured it was just a place that passed people and took their money. But he was so excited about driving.

Six weeks passed, and David wrecked the front right side of the car. When I asked him what happened, he couldn't tell me. I just figured he ran over something because there was no police report. I called my mom and told her what happened and I told her I was not getting the car fixed. I wanted him to see it for a while to try and remind him to be careful and realize he is limited.

David Jon's basketball games, both of the children's choir trips, Dannelle's violin performances, David Jon applying for college, me working, David driving: it was all a lot going on.

On a beautiful April day, nothing special going on, just daily activities as usual, I came home from work, changed my clothes, and stretched across the bed. I was so tired and I was just going to rest for a few minutes before David Jon and Dannelle came in from school.

When the kids came in they came upstairs to our bedroom, a very usual routine since they began driving and I would actually arrive home before them. As David Jon approached the bed-side he said, "Hi, Mom," and I said, "Hi." His eyes then caught a glimpse of something on the floor. He bent down to pick it up and it was the world's tiniest Ziploc bag of marijuana. He asked, "Mom, who does this belong to?" And I was in shock. I couldn't answer him. Going through my mind was, "Lord, why? Why today? Why didn't I see the bag?" I would have given anything to see that before I stretched across the bed. How could I not see what he just came in and picked right up off the floor? I was just quiet and racking my brain.

Because I was non-responsive, he took it and showed it to Dannelle. Dannelle immediately said, "David Jon, you know that's marijuana. We learned that from the DARE drug program at Eakin Elementary." After questioning each other about how this tiny bag got in our house next to their parents' bed they were back to me with questions. I was just spell-bound. They asked again, "Mom, who does this belong to?" I told them, "You'll have to ask your dad." Just as the word "dad" came out of my mouth, we heard the door alarm beep and David was home. Coming upstairs and into the bedroom to see where everybody was, he was greeted with "Hi, Dad," and asked, "Who does this belong to?" He said as best as he could say (due to the aphasia), "I don't know." David Jon asked him again, "Who does this marijuana belong to? "And as he stuttered best as he could he said, "Mine," and pointed to himself.

For the first time ever, I could not cover for David or protect him as I had previously. I could only sit and watch and stare and wonder what would happen next. I was stressed completely out just watching quietly. David Jon asked, "Why do you have this?" And he shrugged his shoulders as if to say, "I don't know." The children looked at me and asked, "Why does he have this?" By that moment, I told them their dad had been on marijuana since I met him. Dannelle cut into the conversation and said, "You, my role model, a dope head?" She was screaming all her words as she spoke, "I can't believe this! I have friends that I try to role model for, but now I find out my dad is a dope head! How?" She asked, "This is just a sinful shame! Who are you?" David was just speechless. David Jon called her several times as she screamed. Once Dannelle was quiet, David Jon said, "Do you have any more?" He answered, "No."

Not believing him, David Jon began to pull his top dresser drawer out and found four more mini-bags of marijuana. Seeing this, his drug bust continued as he stood and pulled every dresser drawer out dumping all the contents onto the floor. I remember thinking, "Metro Police Department couldn't do a better bust," but I just almost rather it be Metro than my child. But this was a quiet relief for me because I had been hiding his habit for so many years and I had asked him to stop so many times. In the bust he also found a check for forty-five hundred dollars, which had come to him from his retro job disability pay. David Jon took the check and said, "I'm going to deposit this check in the bank. It will not be spent for drugs." He asked me for a deposit slip; I gave it to him and he and Dannelle left for the bank.

David had stood quietly the whole time. When everything fell completely quiet he asked what happened. I answered, "You've just been busted by your own children." I began to say, "I knew this day would come but I didn't know how, when, why, or where; I just knew it would come." I knew once the children got back they would question me. As David began to put things back in his dresser drawers, he continued to ask what happened. He was high then. I just stopped talking and went downstairs to prepare dinner.

As soon as the children got back, they handed me the deposit slip and said, "Mom, don't let Dad take any money out of the bank." They also asked me why I didn't tell them and I just said, "It's not my story to tell." I said, "When you do what you do it will soon come out one way or the other, so I guess this was the time for it to come out." David was beginning to slip mentally, and this was a clear sign that he was losing a little of his control.

That evening, sitting down to dinner was very quiet. All you could hear was chewing and forks picking up food. No talking, just quiet. When dinner was over each child went to his or her room while watching TV. It was not much I could tell David because he wasn't sure about what had happened, and we were all in shock. They were because they had found out about their dad, and I was because they had found out about their dad. The days following were pretty quiet. The children would ask me questions about why and how, and I explained that he spent a lot of unsupervised days during his teen years with parents who had deep-seated issues themselves.

The next day came, and it was so good to greet the job. I knew that there would be less stressful than home. Well, was I wrong. While I was sitting at my desk the phone rang late morning. On the other end, the woman asked for Mrs. Walker. I replied, "This is Mrs. Walker." She identified herself as a bank officer and questioned me about the activity on my checking account. I told her I was not sure what she was speaking about.

She began to tell me that the bank teller was writing checks for my husband in the amount of three hundred dollars every three to four days. He couldn't write so the tellers were writing for him. She also noticed that each time he came in, a man was with him. I remained quiet on the line. When she finished telling me about all the checks, she told me I should talk to my husband. At that point she said, "Please come by the bank, and I will show you the checks I am referring to."

When I got to the bank she had them in order by dates as they were written. She said to me, "Mrs. Walker, when men get sick and they can't hold it together any longer for themselves it shows up in the money." I was quiet. I thanked her for letting me know and I left the bank.

While driving away, all I could do is think about calling Dr. Reddick. I was just nervous about talking to David about money because all he ever talked about was that his mother told him to keep plenty of money in his pocket at all times. He was trying to do this on a disability income, and that just couldn't work.

By the next morning, I called Dr. Reddick and asked him if I could come by and see him, and he said "yes." After arriving at his office and waiting briefly I was called in. Once in his office I explained the whole marijuana bust and the call from the bank. I also told him David didn't seem to be at himself and his smoking was increasing. After sitting and thinking for a while Dr. Reddick said it was time to implement the power of attorney. Dr. Reddick called Dr. Calvin, the neurologist, and explained everything to him. Dr. Calvin wrote a letter confirming that David was no longer able to handle his personal business, and Dr. Reddick's statement said the same.

Once these letters were in my hands, I returned to the bank a week or two later. The bank officer I talked with asked, "Mrs. Walker, have you tried to talk with your husband?" And I said, "Not yet because he is going to be fighting mad when he finds out he will not be able to accesses the bank accounts." Seeing me nervous, she tried to assure me I was doing the best thing for the whole family. I was just sick. I couldn't sleep and just tossed and turned all night. Never before had I come to such a strong decision as this one and I knew it would be tough. People can go through a lot and you can say a lot about people, but you mess with their money and they are a changed person on the negative side. I knew it would be tough, but I knew I had to stand for myself, my children, and him also because I had no knowledge about what the future would hold. I just knew it would be different because differences were beginning to show up every day.

The day came and the bank office called me. She said, "Mrs. Walker, your husband and the man came to the bank today, and we explained to him that he didn't have access to the account. He began yelling and cursing as best he could and the bank guard had to escort him from the bank." She said, "Mrs. Walker, I'm sure he is on the way home; just be careful and call me and let me know how everything is going." I thought, "How can she be so concerned when the man is probably coming home to beat me up or better yet kill me?" I was just shaking. I immediately locked the screen door and explained to the children what the bank officer said. They were on guard. I felt so bad putting my children in the middle of confusion and mess, but I felt peace regardless.

As the main door stood open wide and the screen door locked, the Grand Marquis pulled into the carport. I could see David jump out of the car, and he pulled on the door saying, "Let me in."

I said, "David calm down."

He shouted, "No!" He began to ram his fist through the screen and proceeded to unlock the screen. Dannelle was yelling for David Jon and saying, "Come on! Daddy has busted the screen door out and he's after Mom!" It seemed as if David Jon appeared out of nowhere and, in just short steps from getting close to me, he had pushed his dad in the chair and was telling him, "You ain't gonna do nothing to my mama." He kept telling his dad to be still, and David kept trying to get up. He was out of control. David Jon let him out of the chair thinking he was calm, but David kept fighting so he had to slam him to the floor with his hands behind his back. I told the children I was calling Metro Police.

When the police arrived, David Jon let his dad up. I went out and explained to the officers his reason for being upset. The officer said to him that he should cooperate with his family and asked him to calm down. While one officer talked to him, the other talked to me. I told him if he could just calm down there would be no need for arrest. The officers took our son and asked him to stay around to make sure the evening went quietly. Feeling sure of what they had asked us to do as a family, the officers left. As we all went back inside everyone was quiet and trying to regroup from the incident. David Jon began to talk to his father and asked him to just say he was sorry, and he wouldn't. That evening, the home was quiet even at the dinner table.

By May, David came into the house and took me to the car and pointed to the wrecked side of the car and then he pointed to the glove box. I asked him if he wanted me to get the car repaired and he said yeah. I was so proud that he had done this that I felt, "He is much improved so I will get the car fixed." I told him I would take it in, and he was very happy. With David Jon's graduation just a few days away and we were expecting out-of-town guests I had to get the car in and out of the shop soon.

Graduation day came on Thursday, May 20, 1999. My parents, Aunt Annie, and several friends attended David Jon's graduation. The ceremony I looked forward to for so long was at last here. I felt happy, sad, and just all mixed up. I had gone through so many changes. I was standing and couldn't remember getting dressed. With people all around, I thought for a moment. Time stopped as I sat and stared at my son's name in the program. I was feeling blessed that David was at my side after so many close calls with death over the years. Still appearing a little weak, he was at the graduation, and all I knew was that we had made it thus far. As the graduation processed in, just the music of "Pomp and Circumstance" almost weakened my knees. I was there, but I was in total awe. No one knew that I had prayed so hard for us to see David Jon to get to graduate and it was here and now and the music was being played. This was just too much. I just wanted to march in with them, but I remembered I had to just stand quietly and watch all the events. Following the order of the program I kept watch to see how David was doing. I could feel him being so proud, and he was just a glowing dad. My parents and Aunt Annie looked on proudly, too. The first grandson was graduating and their fourth grandchild to graduate high school. Many prayers had gone up for David Jon and, bless his heart, he was all smiles and really didn't know how the prayers of many people had brought him through.

The time came in the program for the graduates to present roses to the special people in their lives, and every graduate had ordered roses to pass out to the people who meant a lot to them. David Jon gave a rose to me, his grandmother, Claudia, and his sister, Dannelle. I could feel the disappointment in David's spirit because he didn't get recognition. I felt so sorry for him but too much had happened between David and his father—and finding the marijuana in April didn't help him at all. David Jon even showed him the rose as if the quiet treatment wasn't enough. I felt sorry for David because I would sit and talk to David often about giving more time and attention to his children. He just wouldn't try and make it better and by now, with his illness, I'm not sure he could make it happen. As graduation continued, I could feel his hurt over his son's act, but I couldn't let this situation steal my joy. At the conclusion, parents were greeting one another with such joy of coming to a completion. We all shared the same joy. As we all hugged and exchanged comments, I realized that we had come to the close of a twelve-year venture. Walking to the car even students were hugging us and excited. As my parents and Aunt Annie got into the car, I could only wonder how proud they felt for they had seen many in the family graduate.

Arriving at home, we had decorated for a graduate dinner, and the excitement continued. Daddy had made his all-famous bar-b-que chicken and ribs and we had all the trimmings. Some of our friends just wanted to come to the graduate party because they knew my dad had the famous meat. As friends began to enter, the home was full of laughter. Again my mind would pause in disbelief that we had come this far. All I could say under my breath was, "Thank you, God," while fighting the tears back. We all gathered around for prayer and, as best David could, he said the prayer. Everyone understood his aphasia by now.

We talked and mingled, and people were eating the bar-b-que like there would not be another meal. Stacey, a family friend, was videotaping and snapping pictures. She was always geared up for family occasions. After more sitting, talking, eating, sitting, talking, eating we began to clean up as people began to leave. Dannelle was so helpful in seeing people out. Nearing the last person, Dannelle screamed, "Mom, come here quick please! Mom, quick please." I didn't rush because it didn't sound like a major "quick please." Once I reached the carport, Dannelle pointed to David's Grand Marquis and he had wrecked the car again where they had just repaired it five days before. I could only laugh and scream because it was hit in the same location where the repair was made. I said, "David, what is it that you are hitting and whatever it is, surely you have knocked it in the ground by now?" I could only laugh. David was looking at Dannelle angrily because she had told on him. Dannelle was always telling on her dad so here she had another grand opportunity.

Saying goodbye to many who had stopped by and finishing cleaning the kitchen, I was still in shock that my older child had graduated and I was so proud of him and glad to seize the moments. Through it all, his dad was there to see it no matter what had happened. The year had been a most difficult one, but we had a joyous event.

The day after graduation David Jon looked for a summer job and registered for summer school. Dannelle always signed up for various summer programs and bible camp. She had pretty much planned her whole summer. David Jon eventually took a job at UPS as a truck loader. The pay was great but he often said loading a thousand boxes is a bit much.

Summer was in full swing, and I was at work greeting in-service planning and packing sacks for individual schools. Summer is hard because we prepared for the fall opening of school. Each minute counted, and you're busy in every minute of every day. You just keep going and you know it will get done.

As Father's Day approached my brother Matthew called to ask me if I would ride home with him to see Daddy for Father's Day. I said I would. He told me he would pick me up on Friday. Getting off the phone I announced that I was going home for Father's Day, and everyone in the family wanted to go so I called Matthew back and he told me to rent a van. We had a wonderful trip home, and Daddy was so excited to have most of his family around him. After talking, eating, joking, and much fun we headed back. Mom told me she would see us Monday because she was coming to Nashville with a friend while she had dental surgery. I told her to drive carefully and we looked forward to seeing her on Monday. Getting up early as usual for work, I was feeling a little tired from the weekend but just as so many other tired days, I just put one foot in front of the other and kept moving.

Mom got to my house about 11:30 A.M. I told her I would see her about 2:30 P.M. or so. As I drove in the driveway David was leaving in his car. It was the first time I had seen him that day since morning. He said (as best he could), "I'll see you later." When I asked where he was going he just said, "Later." I went into the house after he drove away slowly, remembering the fatigued look on his face. I saw Mom and hugged her tight because even though I had just seen her at home it was so good to see her again. She was picking and cooking greens, and we just worked and talked all evening.

Periodically, Mom would ask where David was and I would say, "He will show up after a while." By 10:00 P.M. we were watching the evening news as it went off I told Mom I was going to bed and she asked, "You're not going to wait up for David?" and I said, "Mom I've got to work tomorrow; he will be in sometime." David Jon and Dannelle stayed up while Mom and I went to bed.

By morning, waking to my alarm, I got up and got dressed as usual. Ever since David had the strokes, he would not sleep in bed; he would sit up in the recliner and sleep and maybe lie in the bed after I left for work, so I was not alarmed that he was not beside me. Going downstairs, the TV was not on as usual and David was not in the recliner nor was the car under the carport. I walked back upstairs and told my mom that he didn't make it in. As she was getting out of bed she asked me what was I going to do and I told her, "I've got to go to work. If he doesn't show up in twenty-four hours I will call the police." As I proceeded to walk back downstairs, the phone rang and it was the Metro Police. An officer on the other end of the phone asked if I was Deborah Walker and if David L. Walker was my husband and I answered "yes." He said, "I have your husband here at the corner of Clarksville Highway and Kings Lane as he is passed out in the car." I told the officer I would be right there. I went upstairs and woke David Jon up, and as he got dressed I told Mom to just rest and I would call her later to let her know what happened.

We reached Starvin Marvin, the market parking lot where he was passed out just as the officer said. The officer thought he was drunk, but I could look at him and tell he had a gran mal seizure. He had thrown up and urinated on himself. Everything in his pockets was in the floor of the car, and he was sitting on the passenger side of the car that he was driving when I saw him last. My neighbor who was throwing the early morning paper saw us and told the officer, "This man has been sick for a year; please let them take him to the hospital." After hearing this, the officer said okay. David Jon got in and drove as I followed him straight to Centennial Hospital. Once there, the attendants helped him into the wheelchair, and David Jon left to have the car cleaned due to it smelling so bad. Once inside the emergency room, we repeated the routine we had gone through so many times. We waited for a room and then we got upstairs. I always told them not to publish his room in the directory.

As we settled into the room, the phone rang and it was Walter asking how his boy was. I told him that he was the most low-down human being inside of mankind to leave him in the car alone and sick. I told him to leave us alone and stop calling, and I hung up on him. I just despised the man because he just would not let go. He was tied: sex and drugs were two things they shared. I was just sick and tired.

Once he awakened, I told him what happened. He couldn't believe it, but I told him look at where he was. He was just surprised. I told him, "Well you're back to six more months of no driving because when you have a seizure you have to wait six months before driving again. He just began to say, "No, no," I kept saying, "Yes, yes, no driving."

After going for many diagnostic tests as to what caused all this, the nurses said that in his lab work his THC levels were high. I asked what that was and they said they would have to look it up. After looking it up, the nurses called me to the front desk. They were laughing and I couldn't understand why. I said, "What is it?" and they said, "The THC level is the amount of marijuana in the bloodstream, and he has elevated amounts, which is probably what caused the seizures." I could only shake my head. I went back to the room after thanking the nurses for the information. I told David that we found out what caused the seizures. I told him the THC level was the amount of marijuana in the bloodstream. He said with wide big eyes, "No." I said

"Yes." You can't lie on a blood test. The room was quite quiet and he just stared at me. I told him, "Honey, I've protected you a long time but this is in your medical record and there isn't a thing I can do about it. This is all on you." When Dr. Reddick arrived he just repeated pretty much what I had told him. I could tell he was frustrated with him because he had asked him to stop smoking a long time ago.

We spent two days in the hospital and checked out. Home once again without car keys, he was madder than ever. He began to walk off, and strange people would bring him home. He could not accept his own limitations and failing health.

The summer 1999 was exciting because David Jon was getting ready to enter his freshman year at Tennessee Sate University. There were things to buy in getting ready for going to college. He worked at UPS in the evening and took one class in summer school during the day. His schedule was full. Dannelle traveled periodically on short trips so she had a small agenda, and work was as usual.

David continued to walk off from the family and was never available much to help pick out things for the inside of our new home. Every time our contractor would come, he always asked about my husband and I would say, "It's okay. We can go ahead and look at what you want to decide on." Most of the time David would be out on the streets, and people would call to say they saw him. I would always thank them, and my heart would always be concerned about his safety. Whenever he would make it home late, he was always hungry. I would get out of bed, no matter how late, and fix a meal for him. He would be so hungry he could hardly wait for me to get it together. Knowing he was high and had the "munchies," I always gave him a tossed green salad to keep him from just grabbing anything and risk his blood sugar becoming elevated. I would just sit quietly with him while he ate. Once finished, I would clear the table and he would go and sit down in the recliner with the TV on and sleep. He was in for one more night, and I was glad. For the remainder of the summer, this was pretty much the routine each evening. The children seemed to be adjusting, and they were watching me closely to see my every response to each situation. They knew their dad was struggling and I was too, just trying to keep a level of normal routine for us. His being gone each evening didn't seem to bother the children much because they had grown up with him at classes, rehearsals, dinners, and other evening special functions. And besides with David Jon graduated and Dannelle a teenager, sometimes we would all be gone.

Nearing opening of school I got a call from Miss Margie saying that she could not sit with David any more. She said he had gotten too mean and was asking her to drive him to strange locations. I can remember saying, "Lord, what am I going to do now?" With no one at home during the day, he and his drug partners would be all over my house. I prayed and said, "Lord, just help. I don't know how, who, or where; I just need your help."

God is so good. Just as I was planning to take our son to college, my forty-seven-year-old sister, Reetta, asked if she could come and live with us. I thought, "Lord, this is just what I need; another person to live in the midst of all this instability." But what could I do and what choice did I have and was this from God? I didn't know but she was on her way. No one in my family knew about David's full condition, but I thought I had to tell her since she would be in the home with us.

Upon her arrival, I knew it would be stressful coming to live with us. She was a very gifted individual who just wanted to live and be happy. I thought, "Okay, God, strengthen me okay for the road ahead." After a few days passed, my sister could see visibly that David was in poor health. She began to question and I opened up and told her he was bisexual and was also HIV-positive. She immediately began to say, "I knew he was gay at the wedding but I just didn't say anything and the reason you couldn't see it is because you just didn't know any better. I knew it." She finally got quiet and just looked at me and then said everything would be all right.

Moving day came for David Jon with lots of mixed feelings. He would quietly tell his sister he really didn't want to live on campus, while in front of us saying he was excited about the dorm life. As we began to get all the college dorm gear together, we were truly family helping family on moving day to the dorm. David, myself, Dannelle, and yes, Aunt Reetta, helped to move to the dorm. Just as a mother would, I "Cloroxed" the whole room down to make sure he started off in a clean environment. He had plenty of cleaning supplies too. I put sheets on the bed while he hung his clothes in his closet, and everyone else teased and just looked on. After much cleaning I felt satisfied to leave him in the dorm. I agreed to pick him up on Fridays after work and let him drive the car until Sunday at 6:00 P.M. He was happy with that schedule.

On the way home in the car no one said much of anything. I guess everyone was wondering how it would be to live without David Jon at home. He was a lively person and kept excitement going all the time. I didn't really go through much anxiety about his leaving home because I had gone through so much by now. I was happy to see David Jon get out away from the home especially after experiencing a few incidents. That evening, things were quiet at home, and we all did what I guess we would normally do. It was not hard but after about a month, we had made the adjustment.

Reetta moved into David Jon's room and I began to sleep in Dannelle's room because of David's unstable behavior. With him roaming the streets, I didn't know where he had been or who he might have slept with, and I surely didn't know what creatures were crawling on their bodies or his. I just didn't want to take the chance. Out of his meanness, David would also come into the bedroom at night and turn the music up real loud, and I could not sleep. This forced me to sleep in my daughter's room for the last months we lived on Timothy. Even though it was tough, I slept in her bed, and each night he played loud music. This is when I learned to sleep through noise. David was coming home less and less, more and more. When he would finally come in he would be high and hungry. Often I would get out of bed after long days of work tired and fix him something to eat. Handing him his plate he would sit in the recliner and eat while watching TV and afterwards fall asleep. After the July 1998 stroke he rarely slept in the bed but if he knew I was in the bed, he would turn the music up high. I was a regular in my daughter's bedroom. I would often tell her it wouldn't be like this always, and she would say with a big smile, "It's okay." Dannelle understood, and she appeared glad that I bunked with her each night; however, there were times when she wanted to be alone, and I respected that. Besides I had never slept in the bed with my mother ever before I left home. Dannelle and I have a special bond because of that. She just seems to understand and just goes on no matter what. I think she was into being the only child at home, so nothing else mattered much.

We attended football games and many other college activities. The fall was going well until our former pastor Isaac Barnes was being inaugurated as president of the local seminary school, and David and I decided to attend. David's anger was still shaky and unsure. I asked Dannelle to drop us off, and I told her I would call her to pick us up. The program was wonderful and when it ended, we spoke to several people around us. As we were in the lobby, I took out the cell phone and asked Dannelle to come and pick us up. David saw me on the phone and approached me angrily saying, "My phone." He was having an outburst in the middle of the crowd. I just stepped away because I had seen him like that before and I didn't want him to embarrass himself in front of a huge lobby of people. He just kept angry-looking eyes on me.

When Dannelle arrived, we saw the car and got in. I sat in the back seat while David sat in the front of me. As Dannelle began to pull away, he began saying "phone" louder and louder and turning around in his seat. I said, "David, please turn around; we will talk about this when we get home." He yelled, "No, no!" As he began to yell Dannelle continued to drive but said, "Daddy, stop yelling at Mom and turn around." When she said this still driving the car, he began to try and hit me and Dannelle was yelling, "Stop!" I told Dannelle to stop the car, and he began to hit her. When she stopped the car, I told her I was calling the police. When David heard me say that he jumped out of the car and into the ditch. I got out in my dress clothes and heels and Dannelle got out. I don't know how, but she picked up her Daddy and slammed him on the trunk of the car with his hands behind him. He could not move. The car facing us in the other lane and the car behind us did not move because they had witnessed the whole thing.

When the police arrived, I told them he was upset over not having a cell phone. He and Walter had run the bill up making long-distance calls, and when he had passed out in the car it was found on the floorboard. I decided to keep it before it was lost or stolen because of his current behavior. They had put him in the police car, and I explained to the officer our situation. Dannelle was so upset that I called my friend and pastor's wife, Francis, to comfort her. As the police and I talked, I told them it was no need to arrest him. I felt that if they just let him calm down, he would be okay. Francis overheard our conversation and offered to let him spend the night with her and her family. David got in the car with Francis, and I drove Dannelle home and got her settled. I left the house and went to Francis's house to take David his medicine. Pastor Barnes tried to talk to David, but he would not listen. After the night was getting longer and we could see we were not getting him to act rationally, I left and went home.

David drove a new car every two to three years, wore expensive clothes, ate out at all the best restaurants and attended movies and operas, and purchased just what he wanted. He was a big spender, and we were in debt from credit card usage. He was crying out because his income had been cut due to job disability and illness. For everybody who would listen, he would tell them I had taken his money. I tried often not to talk about him but I would have to tell the story when he was painting a negative picture of me. After all, we were in this mess because of his lifestyle choice. He was irrational and would not listen to anyone. Months and months went by with me picking him up all through the night or nights when he wouldn't even come in at all.

On Monday, October 4, 1999, Francis talked with David and it was a major breakthrough, we thought, to get him to stay at home. It only lasted a few short days. October 11 through 14, 1999, David was staying with Steven and Dorinda Cole. By Monday, October 18, 1999, David was so sick I had to admit him to the hospital. He was so sick that he let me dress him completely. He was dehydrated and weak from being out of his environment. I called to tell Steven and Dorinda that I put David in the hospital, and Steven said they took a gun from David and that he had thrown it in the river. Steven said he was afraid for our safety. I was not afraid because I knew David, and even though he was mad about his declining health and decreased income, he knew I was there for him. When I went to the hospital, I asked David about the gun in front of the doctor and he denied having a gun. I believed him. He was visibly disturbed by this accusation and I knew Steven had lied because he was a dope head. Home from the hospital David continued his visit to the Coles. I was so drained by it all that I decided to write them a letter hoping it would change the situation.

10-27-99

Dear Steven and Dorinda,

I would first like to thank you for being kind to David and showing your love in such a special way. I really appreciate the two of you and our friendship over the years.

Recently there has been some conflict in our friendship and I hope you will allow me in this letter to express my concern.

I want to say to you first that there are always two sides to every story. My story is that currently, my husband whom have I have loved for twenty-two years, is sick and I am doing the very best I can for him. All of us will be given a time to help our spouses and loved ones and right now I am helping mine. I have David under the care of the best doctors Nashville has to offer and I have gone to every doctor visit with him for the past twelve years. I can't begin to recount all of the hospital visits I've been on but it's all about loving and caring for your spouse. Through all of this I have worked daily, kept my house clean, provided meals, counseled teens, and cared in many other areas. God has my plate full, and I am serving him through serving what he has placed me a steward over. Dorinda, you told me do not try to be a martyr for the people. God has put me as a steward over them, and if I can't be a martyr for them, who will? Dorinda, I need encouragement and I am encouraged even though the road is tough. Steven, you lied and you said you feel like a villain. I do know that lying is not right. Steven, you and Dorinda caused me extra stress over what I already have to deal with day to day. Right now all I need is encouragement to stay the course and keep helping and working with my husband and family. I still can't understand how such good friends would lie and cause undue stress to another friend. Steven and Dorinda, I would never in life try and purposefully put a wedge between the two of you. When it comes to our spouses we each know our own. Right now the doctors have explained to me and the family what behavior to expect. Even before they told us we knew that my husband was used to having things go his way or it would not go at all. When they told him he couldn't drive we've had bad behavior ever since. He's told those who would listen that he is angry at God and everybody. I realize it's not about me. Just think, when David could drive a little after the stroke, did he come to your house then? You see, David will use you and when he realized that your house was one block from the bus, he knew he could get a ride home. If he felt you could do anything he wants, he will be your friend; however when you say no or won't agree with him, he is through with you. You can't put family down and you can't put friends down. No matter how bad the picture looks, someone has to be there. I am going to hang in there with my husband. The last year and a half has been quite challenging, but God has given me the strength I need to keep going. When you marry it's for better or for worse so maybe we're dealing with the worst now. But even when things seem worse we must continue to be encouraged and pull everybody along with the family. I understand David and I understand where he is right now and please know that I, his wife, and his children and the extended family are doing all we can for him. Steven, I apologize for being angry but you caused me more stress than I need right now, if you could just understand what I am going through. Lots of times people always take care of the patient with love and concern, but few look at what the caregiver is going through. Dorinda, I apologize for any way I may have been angry toward you, but you, too, caused me stress that I just don't need right now. I pray that you both can forgive me because I have forgiven you. Please understand that the David we once knew is no longer, so we all feel a sense of loss and for one who has known him, I hurt really bad, but it's nothing more we can do. It's all in God's hand. I hope we have all learned there are two sides to every story, I hope we will learn to help each other and not cause stress to one another and we need to understand both sides before we react.

May God Bless You and keep you always.
Your Sister in Christ

I just kept praying that David would get settled in his behavior. Due to Steven and Dorinda's strained relationship, her parents came and took her to live with them. Steven lost the house, so David was back home again because he had nowhere to sleep. He seemed lost, but soon he had met a gay man named

Benny who was also HIV-positive and slow mentally. He would sit with him and I would pick him up at Eighth and Garland. Then he wouldn't call, and then soon he was carrying his overnight bag over. Benny said he had been trying to get David to come home but he just wouldn't listen.

Focus, Focus, Focus:
Signing Up for Disability

Months and time were passing on after David's first stroke. After three weeks in the hospital with David, I had given myself a timeline. I would sign David up for disability by December 1, 1999, if things did not begin to turn around. I kept this thought in the back of my mind because I knew I would have to make a decision if David did not improve. As the months began to roll by we were sent to Vanderbilt Stallworth for speech therapy and occupational therapy. David thought the therapy sessions were "beneath" him, and he would not participate with the therapist because of this attitude. He responded well to the occupational therapist because she kept speaking about learning to drive again. Little progress was made in speech therapy, and they explained to me that the most improvement would come in the first six months after the stroke. After that they could not promise anything. As I was answering the phone at work, which is a part of my morning routine, David Jon called to say his dad had fallen out of bed. I asked him if David was passed out and he said no. I told him I would call Miss Margie and be home right away. Miss Margie added support in the home. She met me at the house and, while I helped David get dressed, she talked with the children. Miss Margie is a God-sent angel, a quiet woman who does not react but acts when needed; just calm.

Helping David to the car, I knew and suspected he had had another stroke. The ride to the hospital was quiet. All I could think about was Dr. Reddick saying, "We've just got to get over the bump in the road." Our bumps seemed to be getting taller and we were not getting over them. In the emergency room they rushed him to the X-ray area for a CAT scan. The results showed another stroke; however, a light one. Dr. Reddick came in and talked to us. He said he would let us go home and asked that I continue to observe him closely. Before leaving, he increased his high blood pressure medication and we went home.

Observing throughout the morning, I felt we could go to afternoon therapy. He continued to have little to no improvement, so I called Lynn at David's job and set up an appointment to go over David's benefits. Lynn was very good at explaining what I needed to do and very sympathetic also. The paperwork I needed to complete seemed endless. I listened carefully and she left the room, giving me ample time to complete David's disability at work. Medical disability paper work even affects medical insurance paperwork. The paperwork was so extensive that I thought often I needed a doctorate to fill it all out. I knew the livelihood of the family was depending on me, so I read each item carefully and fearfully. When you are handling someone's personal business for them, it's important to put yourself in their place. I wanted to make the best possible decisions. I was truly fearful and trying to make sure I was completing everything on David's behalf properly. Because his mental ability at the time was slow, he could not process his personal business. After spending about an hour, I completed the paperwork and thanked Lynn for her help. She said she would be in close touch with me soon.

November came and I was still looking for signs of improvement. The situation remained the same. I explained to David that his six months of sick leave would soon be up, and we would have to prepare financially for down the road. I called Social Security Disability and set up an appointment with them as Lynn had instructed me to do. They told me to come by. When I stopped by, they gave me a long, detailed green form to complete. I remember thinking to myself, "How do people who need help get it without someone to help them complete the paperwork, especially if they can't complete it for themselves?" This form was twelve pages in length, and I carefully completed each question.

They called me in December 1999 and told me to come

in on December 21, 1999, for our appointment. She told me to bring my form in completed. I explained everything to David. He was angry and really didn't want to hear the term *disability* used around him.

We had gone to counseling sessions with a licensed social worker, and because of the limited speech, she was unable to get through to him that his health was not improving. He was in total denial up to this point, and life was changing too fast around him. He was in disbelief about the situation he was in. He was so used to doing just what he wanted to do, when he wanted to do it, and this disability thing was limiting his options.

When I explained to him we needed to go for our appointment with Social Security, he was so frustrated about going. Little did he know, I was just as frustrated. I felt we were going to accept a handout after we had worked so hard on our jobs to do well and progress. When I drove up to the Social Security Administration building, he didn't even want to get out of the car so we sat there quietly. After several moments of silence I told him, "We've got to go in." We both got out of the car, went in, and took a number. When we sat down we noticed all kinds of people in the waiting area with us. Soon our name was called, and we went in to see the Social Security counselor. We both sat down. She was friendly and spoke. I said to her that this was the last place we want to be, but life's circumstances had brought us to here. She said, "Don't worry; I know you're not looking for a handout, but these are dollars you have already paid in." I handed her the completed application, and she typed it all into the computer. She asked very few questions because I had completed the form correctly. She explained to us before we left that we would hear from the disability determination office within forty-five days.

On February 8, the phone call came asking us to come in and sign the final paperwork before the benefits began. I was so relieved because I was just trusting God to lead us. The amount we received allowed us to continue in our current lifestyle without any frills. I thanked God because the family was depending on me. It was important for me to keep focused. There were so many distractions that I thought I wouldn't be able to make it. Just putting one foot in front of the other and just doing what I knew I had to do is what kept me moving.

David was so uncooperative in every way. He was dissatisfied with life and the way things were going. I couldn't take the blame. I could only work in the situation to make it as comfortable as possible. David's mind was on everything totally the opposite of what it should be. As the days went by he was more and more hateful and mean toward me as if I had caused all this. He was so accustomed to things going his way, and by things literally falling in my lap to handle, he was highly upset. I would tell him often, "This is not what I want, but the lives of four people have been damaged, and I refuse to let one person take three people down. No matter how you behave, life has got to go on as best as it can because I have worked hard, loved hard, and kept the faith. I am going to do what is right no matter what your behavior is." I had to look at the whole picture and you can't remove people out of your picture. When that happens, you just have to roll up your sleeves, work and fight on and keep your focus even when others are not helping you and purposefully trying to do everything in their power to bring you down. Thank God for disability because it has sustained us financially as a family unit.

The Courage to Build

On a hot summer August day that we had been anticipating since 1996, we truly made a groundbreaking decision, which was to build our last home. We were excited, so very excited. We decided to build in the midst of a very uncertain future. David felt that if he was going to die, he could at least leave his family in a better dwelling. He was very mixed about building from scratch because we knew very little about the process. Once we came to the decision to build, there was no turning back. Little did I know, it was going to be tougher than ever.

We signed papers in 1996, but because our builder did not have his operation together or was working on other projects, it kept putting us behind in beginning the project. As time passed on, all I could think about was David's gradually failing health, and I would pray that God please let him live to see the project to completion and enjoy the fruit of his labor.

In May 1999, we got a call from the bank asking us to come and update our application. We were excited; however, David began to show signs of not wanting to go through with the project. He knew we had completed the necessary paperwork, and he knew we had come a long way. Some days he was for the house, telling people on the job and in our circle of friends, and then there were times when he was like, "I'm not sure we should do this." Seeing him in this state of mind, I knew it was not quite like him, but I just couldn't understand why or what his insecurities were about. He was happy on one hand because we had good credit and qualified, but underlying, I knew his mind was going back to his mother's statements.

I remembered, before his mother passed, on a visit to Memphis we took the actual floor plans for our new home. I went through each room showing my mother-in-law what it would look like while David looked on. I told her the guest suite was just for her and when she got ready to come and visit or live with us, this was her space. She showed little or no excitement. Later she came to me and said, "Deborah, I've been in this house since James, my husband, died, and he died here and I'm still here." She said, "You all don't need another house because you will begin to act like you've forgotten where you came from. I just don't think you need that house." When she said this to me I thought, "This is why David doesn't want to move, because she is not encouraging us at all."Understanding her mentality, it made me all the more determined to complete the blessed project that my husband and I decided together to do. Besides, my mother-in-law had no idea that we were walking in faith and going against the grain. She had not one clue of the disease and didn't know how much it was telling us what we couldn't do. I could only see in my mind after my conversation with her, "What if Harriett Tubman never came to help free people through the Underground Railroad? What if the land grant colleges had never been built? What if we never moved forward because of another's lack of progressive mentally? We would all still be in straw houses." For me to build this house was nothing more than to show how great and awesome a person can work when and while under tremendous pressure. I know one would think that my plate was just too full, but because it was a full plate, that is what strengthened me to go on. My husband was a very proud, prideful man, and he wanted the house. It was so much a part of him, but because of his mother's haunting words and undiagnosed neuro-syphillis, I just couldn't understand his unawareness. When we made a decision, he always stood by it. I had never seen this type of behavior before in him. After the visit, he never said anything to me about what his mother said to him. As time went on, the contractor began to call us to tell us groundbreaking would be soon, so we continually waited patiently.

My mother-in-law passed before the home was completed.

August through November 1999 was very busy. The house project began to pick up again in August 1999 after firing the first contractor for lack of attention to the project. God blessed me and sent an angel named Sarah Palmer, who held my hand through the process. Sarah was experienced and could see where my first contractor was taking advantage of me in ways I couldn't understand because I understood very little about the home construction. "It's nothing like experiencing it for yourself." She would tell me a lot of what to expect, and we were on the phone daily. I even met the bank president, and he was helpful also. They wanted my home completed, and they were going to see it through. Fred Harp of Homeland Builders came to me and said he could finish my home. He was an angel too because he truly turned the inside of our house into a wonderfully simple home feeling peace within each room. We would fight often over what things cost, and I would tell him over and over that I didn't have any money and he would figure out a way for it to be done.

David was able to help select all of the plumbing fixtures, kitchen and bathroom cabinets; after that he was not around when decisions needed to be made. Dannelle picked out all of the lighting fixtures throughout the home and David Jon had drawn the floor plan that the family worked on before it went to the architect. This was total family involvement even though the disease was an underlying stress.

The new home offered everything David and I needed to do on the first floor. There were handicapped-height toilets in all the first-floor bathrooms. I wanted this home to be very easy to operate in because I couldn't tell what or where we were headed medically. I just knew it would give everyone the space and comfort that we needed for the long run. As I pressed forward, the pressure mounted.

After months of struggling between David's behavior, work, children, David Jon in first year of college, and my sister living with us, the house was just about ready.

I knew if God had brought me from July 1998 to December 1999 it was for us. He just meant it for us.

After much prayer, we moved in December 16, 1999, a day I will never forget. The family moved. With the help of my contractor, David Jon's college buddies, Dannelle's friends from school, and my sister, we made it to 8562 Pleasant Circle. David knew it was moving day so he got up early and left so he wouldn't participate. After moving in and setting up everything, turning the bed back for him, David Jon went back to the old house on Timothy and waited for his dad to come so he could bring him to the new home. David didn't realize that it wasn't his rebellion toward moving. I was thanking God that he was still alive to walk into his new home whether he liked it or not. God had moved in such a miraculous way. I had asked God to just let us move from house to house, and He did. Most people would sell their homes first. Live in an apartment, build, and then move. We moved house to house.

I was, on that day, just in a daze. You see, when God moves, he can fix it where you just can't talk, you can hardly move because it hasn't set in yet. The road was as rough as I thought it would be, but I realized for my husband, children, and extended family, I stayed on the road to completion. I thank God that He kept me when I was afraid; He kept me when I thought I was about to give up. He sent angels to me, and He opened doors that I couldn't see. Most of all I completed the house project because I wanted to do for my husband what he would do for me if he was not sick. I knew he was sick, and I knew I had to keep focused and keep on keeping on. Daily, when I drove up and pushed the remote control of the garage door opener, I just thanked God.

The Plea

As I sit to pen these pages of this section, it—more than any other portion of this book—is so emotionally painful for me: the hurt, pain, anxiety, frustration, trying to keep up, crying, sometimes motionless. This is hard.

Looking back to August 19, 1999, I penned a letter to Dr. Reddick. It reads:

Dr. Reddick,

I am writing to let you know that I have made contact with Nashville Cares. I need help and I have finally realized that helping David to keep his secret is not helping him. I am hoping that the counselor who will do a home visit will be able to help him. He is in total denial about the extent of his illness.

At the present time he is hiding the mail and playing loud music in the home at night. When dinner is served, he takes his plate of food and puts it in the garbage disposal. He continues to walk away from home without anyone knowing it and remains obsessed with money. His communication with family is very limited and his attitude is very poor.

I remain available to help him manage his health and this most difficult day-to-day situation. I will be in touch with you as we progress, because we can't just keep going in the same direction. I am beginning to really feel the burden and weight of everything without help.

Thank you for your continued support.
Sincerely,

Having made contact with Nashville Cares, I felt a small relief was on the way. After making an appointment (August 20, 1999) with Nashville Cares, the local agency for those infected with HIV/AIDS, I met a wonderful counselor named Cindy. Giving her an overview of our family crisis, she was ready to meet with David and asked me if I would meet with her on a weekly basis to continue support for me. I told Cindy the same things I mentioned in Dr. Reddick's letter about the behavior. For instance, one evening alone with David, he was saying for two hours, "Money, I want my money, money, I want my money." And I would say to him, "It's okay," and he would only quiet himself for a few minutes and begin all over again. This occurred on a daily basis especially when I came home from work.

Each week I would meet with Cindy, and each week she met with David. She would not discuss with me anything about David; she was only trying to hear how things were going with me. I told her it was a struggle, but because I had my children and work, it always helped me through the day. She was amazed at the strength and my life thus far.

On David's forty-fourth birthday I took him to Dr. Reddick for one of his regular visits. When the nurse came to the waiting area to call us back, he began to act out, saying, "No, no," directing it toward me. At this point I was glad he was portraying this behavior so the doctor could see what the family and I were experiencing. We were placed in the exam room, and he finally quieted himself as the nurse took his blood pressure. When Dr. Reddick came in, he began to show the behavior again. Medically, Dr. Reddick told him that his blood sugar level and blood pressure were elevated. He increased his medication, and we were on our way.

We were scheduled to see the neurologist on September 17, but David was a no-show. I waited one hour for him, and he knew about the appointment. Realizing his behavior was so unlike him, I just didn't know what needed to be done. My nurse friend Francis came by one evening. She checked David's pressure and talked to him. In their conversation, he expressed he was afraid and frustrated. My heart went out to him because I felt the same way. After her visit, we just sat quietly that evening.

Continuing to meet with Cindy, I always gave her updates

about the behavior. I told her we were making it, but it was a constant struggle. Personally, my life was flowing as well as the children's activities. I soon realized that David was seeking a new doctor. I began to try and figure out what doctor he would go to. I remembered in a conversation with Cindy that the Comprehensive Care Center was where AIDS/HIV patients went for treatment. When I called to inquire, they would not talk to me, so finally after much persistence, I met with his doctor and nurse. They were totally confused because of the speech problems and just needed information that he could not provide. They asked me to please take him back to his regular doctor, and I told them that he refused. As they took him on as a patient, they said they could no longer discuss his health with me because of his patient's rights. I was out of an advocate job just with that one step he took. Not knowing his medical plan was difficult. I felt that I was one of the few who were really looking out for David. After years of doctor visits, conferences on his care, meeting numerous doctors, this was it. I pleaded with David, and he felt in control. I knew that was what it was all about, control. He couldn't realize he needed so much help and was refusing it on every hand.

By January a counselor at the Comprehensive Care Clinic was assigned to David, and I was asked to meet with them. Meeting with them was extremely emotionally draining, time-consuming, and frustrating without any solution. He wanted money and told the counselor he liked marijuana and wanted it. He would push the table where we were sitting into my ribs and just jump up and yell, "I don't want you!" Oh, much pain, tearfully much pain. It was all I could do to pull myself out of the chair to get one foot in front of the other. I felt, "All I have done, all the ways of support, and love put in your direction!" I couldn't believe he was yelling this. Oh God, it hurt to the very bottom of my already fragile soul that was so wounded from years of struggle up to this point. These were the days I could only sit and be quiet for about an hour once I reached home.

It was a daily constant struggle pleading with David to stop roaming the streets because of the need to be at home for safety, but he refused to listen. David lacked focus, communication skills, and had poor health. He refused to accept it. Each time we met with Troy Hurst, his counselor, his anger grew worse. I finally told him I just could not bear to see him out of control. It was taking too much out of me emotionally. During a phone conversation, Mr. Hurst suggested I check with my attorney about being conservator for David. He explained the process, but I thought it was more paperwork, and I was already over my head with paperwork. I never pursued his suggestion at that time. I talked to him quite often, and he was so concerned about my well-being. I told him I was just trying to keep my family together.

I got a call early one morning that David's first cousin in Chicago had passed away. I called from work and told my sister I was going to fly with David to Chicago for the funeral. David kept asking what's happening, and I would patiently explain, "Your cousin died and we're going to the funeral." My sister thought I had lost my mind knowing the behavior problems he was experiencing. I took my chances and got on the plane. He was so quiet and cooperative. Seeing his family members was good for him even though he was not able to communicate well. Through most of the funeral, I remained at his side, and he was fine without any outbursts.

Returning home, he began to stay out late again and roam the streets, calling to be picked up at various hours of the night. One evening after work, I thought, "If he is at home I am going to take him out." Since the Chicago trip was quiet, I thought outings would help, so we went to Riverfront Park and sat on the steps. I told him we were going through tough times that I thought we would never face. I cried and looked into his eyes and said, "I miss the old David," and he moved close to me when I said that. I told him I loved him and that I would never leave him and just be there to help him. He smiled and then cried too. The moon reflecting off the water was just wonderful, and we just sat and cried reflecting back. In moments and time, love can cover all hurts and pains; this was one of those moments that we were lost in.

By April 14, 2000, David was into misbehaving again. While I was at work, my sister called to say she was getting ready to take David to the bus stop, and said she heard the doorbell ring. When she answered it, David took the car and left. Considering he had not yet been cleared to drive after his recent strokes, I was holding the phone speechless and just wondering what I could do. Hanging up the phone, I explained to my supervisor at work and she said, "Do what you need to do." I got my co-worker, who didn't question me, and she drove me all over the places I thought he might be. Before long we spotted the car at the Maxwell House Hotel. I remembered that he talked to his old boss about having lunch. As I watched him go into the hotel, I got the car and drove it home.

Explaining to my sister what happened, she drove me back to work. I called his former boss and told him what had happened and asked him to drop David off at home, and he agreed. I knew that my evening would be rough. Knowing that David Jon was good with his dad in adverse behaviors, I went by his dorm room and picked him up on my way home. I briefed David Jon in the car about what had happened. As soon as we walked in, David Jon said, "Daddy, I hear you've been driving today," and David said, "No, no." I proceeded to my closet to undress, and I could hear him asking for the keys. He refused to hand them over to David Jon.

When I returned to the room I said, "David, please give David Jon the keys." I said, "Do I need to call your boss and ask him to come and get the keys?" He said no. David Jon asked again, but with no response, he picked his dad up and sat him in the recliner, crossing his arms, and began searching his pockets. He threw the keys out on the floor and let his dad's arms go free. He said, "Mom, I'm going downstairs to check out these keys."

On his way back up the stairs with his aunt behind him, David jumped into David Jon's arms while on the staircase. With all his strength, David Jon lunged his body forward, pressing his dad into the wall, breaking the sheetrock. I realized this was a wrestling match in progress. David pushed David Jon trying to get the keys back, and they went up and down the hallway pushing. Finally, David Jon picked his dad up and put him in the recliner again, let it back, and left the house. I looked at David and looked at the hole in the sheetrock of my brand-new home and said, "David. all we asked for was the keys." He soon left walking from home.

That same evening when David came home, he was crying. David Jon was already home. David asked David Jon to come to the bedroom. It was at that moment that he told David Jon he was HIV-positive. David Jon looked at me and asked, "Mom, are you okay?", and I said, "Yes, baby." You could tell David was so relieved.

Ann Marie, the psychiatrist, had asked him not to tell the children because of the nature and seriousness of the issue. She felt that they were not mature enough. Getting young people to understand confusing things was difficult, but once again their father's narcissistic behavior took over. He didn't seem to care that they knew.

As you know with brothers and sisters, David Jon told his sister. They both came to me and cried in my arms, asking "why"? In the days to come, I explained to them all that had happened over the years. They called Dr. Reddick and met with him without me or David seeking more knowledge about their new-found discovery of a deep, dark family secret. I told them I had stayed to protect them because we were all innocent. I encouraged them to love their dad because he was the only dad they had, and I told them I had made a covenant before God and company and I was a covenant keeper. "Oftentimes we do things we don't want to do, but we do them because it's the right thing to do at the time. I just want to do right regardless of the issues of others," I said. I assured my children I was steady and was still fighting for the entire family. I let them know, "What rests on your dad has nothing to do with you. You have a whole life ahead of you. You must live for you and must take care of you."

By June 2001, I called Comprehensive Health Care and asked about David's medical plan, and they would not give me any answers. As far as I could tell, the only thing they changed was to add anti-depressants to his list of medications. I even called Dr. Reddick on July 5, 2001, and I realized he had grown weary of our situation. He said, "Mrs. Walker, what do you want me to do, call and harass those doctors? They won't talk to me. I've spent ten years in this. I don't have time, and they won't talk to me; however, I will try and call them and I will call you back."

While waiting to pick Dannelle up from work on July 11, my cell phone rang. Troy Hurst was calling to say that he had taken David to Vanderbilt Hospital. Dannelle and I went to the hospital immediately, and he said he had some kind of infection but did not know. After visiting, we soon left. Strangely, I had peace in my heart just knowing where he was and that I could go to bed at night knowing I wouldn't have to come back out to pick him up.

By the next morning on my job, the doctor who would not talk to me called to inform me that my husband had neurological syphilis. He said the treatment was penicillin through IV for ten days. Again, I had peace because he would be in the hospital for ten days. "I was on real vacation for ten days," I thought, "knowing where he was and not having to pick him up." That evening I pulled up on the Internet the medical information about the neurological syphilis, and it explained why we had the adverse behavior. The report defined neuro-syphillis as an infection of the central nervous system by a virus that destroys brain tissue. It also described symptoms as eye disturbances, tremors, and disordered speech, as well as severe intellectual deterioration and psychotic symptoms. My husband had experienced them all, after thinking back. I called Dr. Reddick and explained David's condition, and he asked me to come in to be tested for syphilis just as a precaution because we didn't know when he contracted it. My test results returned negative.

Once discharged from the hospital, his behavior was a little better but he still stayed out all night or came home late. Still keeping the family together, the children took us to the Rain Forest café for our twenty-third wedding anniversary. The evening was pleasant with light conversation.

It was a normal day. The family as a whole continued in daily activities as normal. By evening, David called and when I picked him up, he had been robbed. His wedding band, his anniversary band, his watch, his bracelet, and his necklace were all taken. The robbers had cut his fingers and the palms of his hands. I cleaned his wounds and bandaged them up. He stayed home two days in a row behind the robbery, and was up and out again on the streets. During these months, we as a family pleaded with David to let us help him. We loved, cared, we bore it with a smile, we lived through hard places due to his irrational behavior.

Let's look at the whole picture: Family—#1 Priority— to make sure everyone is cared for, the "Lie-Bisexual," forgiven, pleading, threatening and The Diagnosis; HIV-positive, which meant no sexual relationship with spouse, adjustment. We've got to hang in there no matter what. Doctor's visits, diabetes, high blood pressure, blood clots, stomach cancer, heart attack, dental problems, stroke, aphasia, neuro-syphillis, and that meant we had to deal with the fact that David could not drive. Plus, with the drug-use habit and illness caused job loss, decrease in income, we purchased a new home, and moved to have every-thing on first floor for medical reasons. Due to loss of income and inability to do what you used to do, you want to leave the family. The family had suffered loss of respect, and uncertain future. All of this seemed too much for anyone, right?

In spite of everything, the family has tried to remain a supportive unit, helping in every way. He wanted out due to the lack of control. There was no need for power struggle. As a family unit, the lives have been affected mentally and emotionally. As the adult looking at the whole picture, we could have operated as a unit with the condition, but David wanted out of the family. He wasn't even looking at the long-term consequences for everyone. Due to my working, the medical insurance from my job was primary, Medicaid was secondary, and his single coverage medical paid last. There were no outstanding debts. All our debts were paid. Pharmacy receipts had to be in dual after each visit for the insurance to cover bills. As a family we have tried to take care of the responsibilities of the family. We didn't need Human Services or handouts.

David wanted to move by himself. I thought, "There is no need for separate housing. This move would cause the family that is grieving already to grieve once more. The family would suffer, once again, financial loss as to separating and duplicating things that are already in place."

The separating bottom line for David was, "I want to do just what I want to do and have just what I want to have. Forget the years the family struggled to get where we are today and forget about the lives I have affected emotionally and mentally." Coming through twenty-four years just doesn't mean anything to someone who just wants out no matter what.

In the spirit of the ancestors, I had to continue to run the race and press forward. Though very tired, I am still holding on, and we must fight on.

Letting Go

After days, evenings, nights, and months of David's behavior toward being home, letting go was the last thing I was thinking about doing. I was a fighter, always one to hang in there. Besides, I had already come through so many issues.

It was July, the summer of 2001. The weather was hot and muggy like most Tennessee July summers. David by now had been walking the streets and lying down in places wherever people would let him. Since October 1999, I still received phone calls in the middle of the night to come and pick him up whenever he would want to come home. Most times he could not tell me where he was, so a person who was with him would take the phone and tell me where to come. David's behavior had become so anti-family, and he did not realize how he was hurting himself, me, and the children. Knowing David Le'ron Walker, his behavior against us proved to be like nobody we had experienced before. David Jon would often say his dad had passed away July 5, 1998 (the date of the first stroke, which left him with aphasia).

David was on the streets and was being given advice by his peers in the streets. Those peers were diseased as he was, and in one particular instance, the person he was endeared to was mentally retarded.

In early July I began to get phone calls from Nashville Cares asking for various documents, like our marriage license, Social Security benefits, and other documents. The one document they consistently called for was David's power of attorney. Dr. Andrew Reddick and Dr. Calvin had implemented the power of attorney in April 1999 because at that time David's behavior was so out of order that it was necessary in order for the family to continue to thrive. With David's narcissistic behavior, he only wanted just what he wanted and had no concern for the family, mentally, physically, spiritually, or financially. He was all for himself. This truly was not the David I had married, the father of my children or the prior responsible person we all knew. We had fully completed our estate planning in November 1994, years before the behavior change. Dr. Reddick ran tests, and he began to recommend psychological testing so David was quite upset. Mentally we could all see he was suffering. As he suffered it was all I could do to keep my own self intact and mind the business of the family.

David was not mentally capable of accepting advice that would help him, always going for advice that was threatening his quality if life as he knew it. It was so hurtful to me watching him fight against the family when prior to the strokes he was pro-family, always wanting us to do the right thing and have everything we needed to thrive. His drug habit, his sexual habit, and his altered behavior were truly taking us in a different direction.

I remember in July my mother was visiting and David came in to say he wanted to talk to me. In the conversation, taking me from visiting my mom, and taking four hours because of aphasia, he told me he had someone who was interested in him and that he wanted to divorce me. I knew then it was these outside influences that was on a higher level than I could even imagine. Sitting there, my heart was so empty just looking at him knowing the condition he was in and thinking to myself, "Where do I go from here? And what can I do to protect myself first in order to be able to protect him and the family? What can I do?"

This question lingered in my mind after he left for another evening on the streets away from family who loved him and had great concern for him. Getting ready for bed that evening I was just emotionally whipped going over in my mind what he had said to me. I was whipped, but what could I do that would help and protect the family at this point? I know one or some may wonder why I wouldn't just divorce and get him out of the family and move on. That's a lot easier said than the impact divorce would have on him. I often explained to David, "We never want to go downtown (meaning through the court system) because downtown is not for the family and would certainly cause us more hurt, pain, and suffering with them making a decision for us without knowing the full history of who we are, where we have been, our accomplishments and ability to swim under hardships that we were experiencing."

David could not realize that his monthly expenses were greater than his monthly income. His medication alone would be three thousand to four thousand dollars a month, depending on what was happening with him medically. He was covered under my Blue Cross/Blue Shield family plan, and I had taken out a single-coverage Blue Cross/Blue Shield medical insurance policy for him to make sure he was covered for the medical and hospital visits. Comprehensive Care Clinic advised me to keep his medical insurance coverage at max because you never can determine the next major hospital visit. Because I am married to him and working daily, Blue Cross/ Blue Shield pays eighty percent out of my policy coverage on him and his pays twenty percent only after my insurance coverage paid. Medicare/ Medicaid would pick up on various things but still did not carry the coverage that Blue Cross/Blue Shield did.

David did not have knowledge that if we divorced, it would render him impoverished. His monthly benefits were too high to approve him for any welfare programs, and AIDS medications are not subsidized. I never wanted to divorce him because I was looking at the whole picture, and he was only looking at himself. He didn't realize I had enough documentation and my story alone would cause any lawyer to turn everything over to me because the doctors had already realized his inability to be rational about his own situation and abandonment for the family. My whole attitude had been, "How can we as a family continue to help him when he cannot realize he's putting himself in a more-threatening position?" I did not want to beat him down when the disease he was carrying was beating him down much more than I could.

That night I slept very little, and when I awoke to get ready for work, all the things he had pieced together to say to me were still on my mind. As my work day passed I couldn't wait to get home to take a nap because I was emotionally whipped and physically tired. As I drove into the driveway I stopped to take the mail out of the box. Thumbing through the mail, I found a letter from some attorney's office addressed to me. Parking the car in the garage and coming into the house, I put my purse and keys down on the counter. David, with the help of Nashville Cares, had been referred to an attorney. This attorney had no knowledge of our history and had drawn up a letter revoking my power of attorney privileges. I could only pull my kitchen table chair out and sit down. He had managed, with his limited communication skills, to convince this attorney to revoke the power of attorney. It was at that moment I had enough. I thought you can't even begin to think about what this will do to him. He was, and I knew, out of his right mind to make rational decisions. I just sat down quietly going over the years of pain and suffering we had already come to, and to come to this made no sense. I figured that David was upset because his weekly allowance was forty dollars a week. Everything was provided for him at home. Meals, laundry, transportation (the doctors had restricted his driving due to seizures). He would give his money to his street friends for favors and drugs. The forty dollars weekly was all the family budget could allow due to his monthly expenses. He just could not understand the whole family has needs, not just one person.

Arising from my chair, I called our family attorney Rickie Slaughter to explain what had happened. I asked her at this point what we would possibly do in our situation. Rickie suggested that I needed to apply for emergency conservatorship, which is higher than a power of attorney. She asked me to come into her office the next day for further consultation. On July 18, 2001, I went to her office and had a conference with Rickie Slaughter and Leah Holland. Leah was a very bright, experienced lawyer in Probate Court-type issues. Because our situation was so unique and we knew there were no easy answers, they worked on the emergency conservatorship for the protection of David and the entire family. Both attorneys clearly understood why divorce was not an option.

After obtaining all necessary information needed to support applying for the conservatorship, it was granted on a temporary basis pending investigation into our personal lives. I had provided my attorneys with documentation that David had been driving a friend's van and I had a check run on the van license plate number only to find out that it belonged to a man with a restricted license, DUI charges, assault and battery charges, and disturbing the peace charges. It was all there. The court saw that David could be taken advantage of or brought into a life-threatening situation. David had no knowledge about what was about to take place and how it would change his life and the life of the family as we had known it.

I didn't know where this would take us; all I knew was that I had given my best days, months, and years as an advocate for my husband, and he could not see the whole picture. I had done for him all I knew to do for him under the circumstances I had been placed under and the situation I was in, trying to pull everybody through successfully. I had to at this point, knowing I was tired, sick and tired, of a consistent situation that beat me down on a regular basis.

It was at this point that I had to let go and let the system that I had fought so long and hard not to come to take over. There was no other way. The very foundation of things the way they were was being shaken. It threw me emotionally into a total tailspin. I had to let go. I told myself over and over, "You've done all of everything you could possibility do. Let it go, let go." I began to cry, and I cried because I felt another piece of me had been taken away, and I had no clue as to what the consequences of the conservatorship would be. After crying more, I still came back to let it go. I had to trust fully the lawyers and their advice and let it go.

Twelve years advocating for an issue is a long time and it was hard to let it go. My attorneys, after hearing my story, respected me and listened attentively to my explanation about why divorce was not an option. Just as all the physicians had told me when I was looking for options, I was stuck in a situation that had no easy answers, and my attorneys also came to the same conclusion. Things moved quickly. Because of the size of our estate and conflict of interest the judge/court appointed the county conservator. My attorneys were pleased with the judge's appointment. The conservator was short in statue and spunky in personality. You could tell she had a lot of cases, but she was getting things in order.

In the coming days, my husband was informed by the court that he had been appointed a county conservator and that he could no longer make business decisions for himself. He could not understand what was happening at all. He thought revoking my power of attorney would give him a divorce from me and put all of his monthly benefits in his control. He just did not understand, and he remained on the streets.

The weekend came, and I asked my son to travel with me to Milwaukee, Wisconsin, to visit a senior relative. I just needed to change scenes for just a brief moment. While away, a car dealer had left a message asking me to call him. I thought, "Why is a car dealer calling me?" My daughter stayed at home, and I would call and check in with her. On our way back from out of town, Dannelle called me on my mobile phone to say her dad was at home and that he was driving a brand-new SUV. I said, "What?" She said, "Mom, it is awesome," and I thought, "He could always buy pretty cars." My attorneys had introduced me to the conservator over the phone, so I had all her contact numbers with me. As we traveled into town, I called her and explained to her what David had done. She said she had been trying to catch him for two days. I told her he was at our home and she could catch him there now.

On our way in, I stopped by the car lot where David had

purchased this car. His credit was good so he did not have to put any money down, and the dealer filled out all of his paperwork for him. A friend was with him the dealer said and helped him do most of the talking. I explained to the dealer that I was not going to pay for that vehicle and I showed him the court documents appointing a conservator over him. He begged me to tell him where David was and told me he would tear up the paperwork if I would just bring the car back. He explained that he had called me because David could not give him any account numbers and income information. In the meantime, we left the dealership and when I arrived, the conservator was in our home and presenting David with his court documents. When she finished talking to him you could visibly tell he didn't understand at all what was happening. The conservator talked with me briefly to let me know that she was taking him to return the car and that she was taking him to her office for further explanation about the days ahead. The conservator told me that my attorneys discussed with her our financial situation, and she asked me to continue with business as usual, however, separating out his half of the expenses.

As time passed David continued to come and go as usual but reporting to the conservator. Mid-September, my attorneys called me with dates for scheduled events to take place. A guardian *ad litum* had been appointed to talk to me, the children, family friends, and doctors involved in David's care. An independent doctor was sought out to give David a clinical evaluation, having no prior knowledge of his condition or history. Once this process was completed we headed to Probate Court. Court was a place I prayed so hard not to ever have to go. We were and had been a very independent family making our own decisions, I just dreaded someone not really understanding the depth of our relationship discussing us and making decisions for us. I had to let that go also.

Getting ready for court that day, I called in sick from work so as to not call attention to my situation in my job place. Most of my co-workers knew that my husband was sick, but they did not know the extent of his illness. I wanted to keep it that way because I knew I could always go and find peace on my job even though days I can't number I had sat at my desk and cried.

Meeting my attorney in the hallway before going into the court, she briefed me on what to expect. David, a Nashville Cares case worker, David's attorney, the court-appointed conservator, and the guardian *ad litum* were all present. I had already been given the report of the guardian *ad litum,* and it was a report indeed. David had confessed in ways from which there was no return. The report described that, upon his interview, David stated that he was "through with" his married life and that he wished to obtain a divorce. He also acknowledged having a physical relationship with a male partner, who was described as a "significant other" and indicated that he took necessary precautions to prevent transmitting his infection. The report also included a statement from David's "significant other" in which he stated that he cared for David and wanted a committed relationship with him, and that he wanted to help take care of him. He also stated that he was afraid others would take advantage of him. I was shocked at what I was reading.

As we entered the courtroom, sitting on opposite sides, I kept feeling I really didn't want to discuss this. Oh, God, I really don't want to be here. As the case before us slowed on, the judge passed to hear our attorneys. The attorneys had gotten together and agreed that the conservator should remain in place and that she work with the family to conserve it also. The judge agreed, and we were on our way.

The conservator told David to locate an apartment, and his car was returned to him. Dannelle suffered emotionally because she had been driving the car and it was suddenly taken away. The conservator was only appointed over his finances and not his personhood. As time continued, he remained without an apartment and continued to come and go for the next three months after the appointment of the conservator. As a family we would go days without hearing or seeing David. We just knew that was the way it was with him.

One Wednesday evening he came over. The children let him in as I had been advised to change the locks on the doors for safety purposes once the courts were involved. He began to visit with the children while I was away at Bible study. I called home to let the children know I was on my way home, and they informed me that their dad was home and he looked like he wanted to spend the night with us. I told them I was on my way. When I arrived, I spoke to David and asked him how he was doing, and he always responded that he was fine. I asked him if he found an apartment and he said, "I have no medication." He had left his medicine at the place where he had been going in and out of and he could not find the persons at home. They were gone, he stated, for the last two days, and he had not had medicine for two days. I got up and gave him the medicine that he had left behind. I even called the apartment building supervisor where he said his medicine was to see if they would unlock the door and get his medicine for him, but they couldn't because his name was not on the lease.

Hanging up the phone, I explained to David what the supervisor said, and he just looked at me. His expression said, "Well, what am I going to do." He asked to spend the night at home, and I got up and left the room. I wanted so much to say, "You can stay; your bed is still intact," because he was still coming and going even though the locks were changed. When I came out of the kitchen, I told him he could not spend the night because my lawyer would get upset, and then I asked, "Where did you sleep last night?" He said he stayed at a friend's, so I told him to call his friend and go to his place. I think, at that moment, for the first time, he truly realized he was out of the home and my long suffering with his situation involved me no more. As he left, I told him to call me and let me know how he was doing, and he did.

On Thursday morning, I called the conservator and

explained to her the events of the past evening. She said to me, "I will have an apartment for him by the weekend." By this time our finances had been separated based on each of our monthly expenses. We were both operating out of whatever income we had separately. I was so thankful to be able to continue without him and the enormous stress and strain. I only realized that the burden had been lifted and the bondage I was under had been relieved by the courts. The courts had actually helped and I was beginning to see. I felt that my attorneys would sell my home because I did not have twelve thousand dollars to pay them in legal fees, but they said they would try to get the court to waive the fees.

Prior to the move on Saturday, the conservator came to our home and sat down with our family and explained David's apartment and asked if I had any furnishings for him. He told the conservator that he wanted all-new furniture, and we both just stared at him. He had no clue about how this arrangement affected his financial picture. She had found a two-bedroom luxury apartment in downtown Nashville with amenities. We were pleased with her recommendations. After she left, I began to help David get his clothing together for the move, and I gathered kitchen and bathroom things I thought he would need. I packed food for him, too. Before we could get things together, he said he had to leave. That's just the way his mind would run. He had no thought for sticking to or finishing what he needed to. He left and I continued to get his things ready for the move to the apartment. I called a trusted family friend and asked her if her brother could come in the morning to help me move something downtown. She talked with him, and he agreed. What was happening to our family was so personal and private and these friends understood and didn't ask or speak a word about moving him.

November 3, 2001, was truly a day of mixed emotions. Many things were coming to an end. An end to David's coming and going, an end to uncertain days and nights, an end to sleeping on a pull-out bed in Dannelle's room, and an end to being the up-close and personal advocate for my husband of twenty-four years. I came to realize a major change had come and I had handled it as intelligently as I could. I breathed deep and said, "You go on, girl, you've got to go on and you have to let go."

That morning David Jon and I met my friend's brother at her home. I asked him to take me to Sam's to get new mattresses. I was giving David our mattresses out of the master bedroom that I had never slept in since we moved into our new home. He agreed to take us, and we were on our way. At Sam's, I found a pillow top mattress set, sheets, and comforter. As we began to check out, my cell phone rang and it was Dannelle calling me to tell me her dad had called and he had the key to his new apartment. I called him and told him I would be there real soon. When we arrived back at home from Sam's, David Jon and my friend's brother set up my new mattresses on the bed frame. I smiled and then we loaded all of David's things onto the truck, and we headed downtown to the new apartment. David and his friend met us at the truck and began unloading. After getting him settled, we returned to the truck to go home. I was so thankful to them for helping us out in this strange situation, but no questions or explanation was required.

The day was just emotionally charged. Dannelle was losing a nighttime roommate after four years, and David Jon would miss our late night TV watching and conversation in his room. That evening, David Jon helped me to put my sheets and comforter on the bed while his girlfriend and another close friend cheered us on. They said, "Mrs. Walker, we are so happy for you to finally [November 2001] get to sleep in your bedroom." I told myself I would sleep on the pull-out mattress until a permanent change of some sort took place. Through this experience I can sleep on basically anything, anywhere. I've learned to be content in any and every situation, believing everything will be all right for me now. My bed is still special. I know it's undefiled.

Time and days have passed, and it's simply wonderful to have a peace within and peace on the outside. Every day I look forward to the newness of the day and seize the minutes, thankful for everyone of them. My and David's relationship now is quite pleasant, and he calls me and stops by to see me often. He always calls before he comes by to see if we're at home. No longer do any of us sit by the phone and wait to see if he will call to be picked up from an undetermined location. When he visits, I often offer him a meal, and he accepts with a smile. To my surprise, by January 2002, he was asking if he could come back home to live with us. I asked him why he wanted to come back because I had let go so he could do just whatever he envisioned doing. I told him he couldn't come back because he didn't want to give up his behavior that had gotten him to this point in the first place. He sat quietly and just smiled. There were no words exchanged and soon he said, "I'm leaving, and I'll call you tomorrow." To my surprise he did call me, and we talked as best we could and said goodbye.

As I began to let it go even more, I realized I have fought a good fight and I've pressed forward and I understand the meaning of laboring love, understand the meaning of "trouble don't last always," and I understand "weeping may endure for a night but joy comes in the morning light," and I truly must continue to run the race because I have miles to go before I hang up my shoes. Letting go was hard, but I believe I've succeeded.

Suddenly and It Came to Pass

In this life we are given, there are many twists, turns, hills, mountains, and, yes, valleys. We are uncertain, on every hand, where we are headed. I've learned that love is most powerful, and it can cover a lot. I've learned never to say "never" because when you are presented with a situation, you can't determine how you will respond until it presents itself. One thing is for sure: there is a response, be it positive or negative; there is a response. Everyone has control over their own actions. Everyone determines what levels they will operate on, and everyone knows when enough is enough and when you are sick and tired of being sick and tired. In my situation, it has created a stronger individual. My family is even stronger, and we have a great sense of accomplishment for striving to keep the family together. As we remain married, everyone is still thriving, healing, adjusting, and discovering each new day with a different level of appreciation. I don't want to romanticize my life; know that AIDS/HIV is real. Because I have truly come through very painful and difficult moments and places, I hope you see that taking the road less traveled will cause you to grow in ways you can't imagine with benefits you can't even explain. For others who are going through similar experiences, just remember that, through not stopping, you are moving. You are moving and remembering when you've done all you know to do, and you let it go, you can say, "Suddenly and it came to pass. It's over!"

Acknowledgments

If one would ask me the question, "How did you come through your storms of life's challenges?" I would say that, in my mind, I was standing between the cross and the slaves. These two things, and the history behind both, kept me focused at all times. Thank you, Jesus, and thank you, slaves, for your inspiration. I realized that I had not hung on the cross and not had nails driven in my hands and feet or worn a crown of thorns on my head. I realized that, like the slave, I was in bondage, but just like Harriet Tubman, I kept continuously moving, working with my husband and children daily, and realizing that if I chose to turn back, then my leading would fail. By moving and working, God was refining me daily in the fires of my tribulations. I had no time to be lazy and out of it. I just had to keep moving.

In the midst of my saga, I want to thank my children, David Jon and Dannelle Walker. If it weren't for their precious smiling faces from infancy to childhood encouraging me, I wouldn't have made it. They encouraged me daily and gave me a reason to keep getting up and going. Those two individuals helped me in the toughest of times with steady quiet spirits and a willingness to keep going in the spirit of order and decency.

Mrs. Malettor Cross, Ladies Retreat speaker, who was the first person I told my situation to and who said stay with him, he needs you now.

To Mary McCutcheon, I want to thank you for being a great companion for my children and for always telling me to hold on during tearful and dry eyes.

Unexplainable thanks goes to Judson Rogers, M.D., who stood at the bedside days and nights, who had special heart-to-heart talks with our children, and who always kept us laughing with his dry sense of humor. To Dr. Mary Anne Blake, his wife, thanks for all the allowed phone calls and notes to your home. You are two awesome doctors.

To nurses Joan and Connie, who listened on every visit and nicknamed me Job, your smiles always made me feel sunshine when things were dark and dreary.

Special thanks go to Dr. Henry W. Foster for counseling with me and the children and helping us to understand our unique situation.

Thank you to Dr. Forrest E and Jackie Harris, who stood by our family and stood watch through so many nights and ministered to us each Sunday and helped us to understand God's unconditional love for us.

Thank you to our longtime friends, Don and Carletha McNeil and Vickie and Wayne Fleming. You always displayed family togetherness and love and shared with us.

Thank you to Bertha Lee for telling me not to cry in front of low-down people and for encouraging me to work toward my goals.

Thank you to Stella Lowe for praying for me and encouraging me to pray out loud.

Thank you to Roxie Johnson, Cordelia Wakefield, and Anna Mundy for praying for me without knowing all of my troubles.

To Thyckla Gray and Robert Johnson, thank you for taking my phone calls day or night and listening and helping me without question. You two truly have blessed me to know that there is another day.

To Ira and Jean Tolbert and Diertra and Kenneth Bledsoe, your kindness will always be remembered.

Thank you so much to Loyce Stewart Thompson for editing my book and inspiring me to publish my story.

Thank you so much Jeanette Holland Sims for telling me that the Lord will restore the years the canker worm tried to take.

Thanks to attorneys Billey Sanders and Lela Hollabaugh and judges Frank Clement and Randy Kennedy for giving me advice and fair judgment.

I want to thank Bishop Joseph Warren Walker III for all of your spirit-filled and anointed sermons that gave me the courage and daily strength to keep on running the race that had been set before me.

Thank you to my mother, Claudia Davis Williams, and my deceased father, Henry Hewitt Williams, for all of their days teaching and training me. Thanks to my beloved and deceased aunts, Annie Mae Miller and Helen A. Oliver, who always lived the meaning of decency and orderliness.

Thanks to my only blood sister, who stood by me and helped me. Thanks to my nieces and my brothers for being there.

Finally and most of all, thank you Lord, the Most High God, for trying me through the fire. May the blessed anointing you placed on me be used to glorify you and horrify the devil. I pray that you will use my testimony to encourage all to seek your most personal guidance, faith, and trust when life challenges them.

May God bless and keep all who hear my story as he has blessed and kept my family and me.

About the Author

D. Felecia Walker is a woman who believes in walking the walk and being a doer. She realized that one person's issue could not destroy the lives of her and her two children. She is a true survivor.

As a professional master's degree-level dietitian, her various positions have enabled her to work with people from all walks of life. Facing life's challenges, one right after another, has given her wisdom that surpasses all understanding. D. Felecia's focused and sometimes serious look often causes people to miss the understanding loving care and concern she has for others. She truly knows it is not about her.

D. Felecia wants to live a legacy that she pressed forward in life when life was bearing down on her so much that she thought it would squeeze the very breath out of her lungs. She says the personal experiences and the things she has gone through and witnessed in life have made her who she is.

D. Felecia is strong, resilient, courageous, full of life with joy overflowing and beautiful inside and out. She presses forward with a spirit not to press is the most motionless place to be in. To keep moving, pressing, and forging the way through, offers many adventures on the journey.

I must press forward.

This is D. Felecia Walker's legacy.